women

& social transformation

Studies in the
Postmodern Theory of Education

Joe L. Kincheloe and Shirley R. Steinberg
General Editors

Vol. 242

PETER LANG
New York • Washington, D.C./Baltimore • Bern
Frankfurt am Main • Berlin • Brussels • Vienna • Oxford

Elizabeth Beck-Gernsheim, Judith Butler,
and Lídia Puigvert

Women
& social transformation

Jacqueline Vaida, Translator

PETER LANG
New York • Washington, D.C./Baltimore • Bern
Frankfurt am Main • Berlin • Brussels • Vienna • Oxford

Library of Congress Cataloging-in-Publication Data

Women and social transformation / Judith Butler ... [et al.].
p. cm. — (Counterpoints; vol. 242)
Includes bibliographical references and index.
1. Feminist theory. 2. Feminism. 3. Sex role. 4. Social change.
I. Butler, Judith. II. Counterpoints (New York, N.Y.); v. 242.
HQ1190.W673   305.42'01—dc21   2003011839
ISBN 0-8204-6708-1
ISSN 1058-1634

Bibliographic information published by **Die Deutsche Bibliothek**.
Die Deutsche Bibliothek lists this publication in the "Deutsche
Nationalbibliografie"; detailed bibliographic data is available
on the Internet at http://dnb.ddb.de/.

Published by arrangement with El Roure Editorial, SA

Cover art by Colin Myers
Cover design by Lisa Barfield

The paper in this book meets the guidelines for permanence and durability
of the Committee on Production Guidelines for Book Longevity
of the Council of Library Resources.

Printed in the United States of America

Contents

ROSA VALLS

Preface

I begin writing these lines filled with emotion from having recently read the chapters of this book, which sets out an international feminist debate that is as original as it is interesting. The dialogue between Butler and Puigvert is not of two positions stuck in the typical twentieth-century proposals; rather, both authors are transformed in relation to the other's contributions. In this way they coincide on the emphasis they give to dialogue, understood as that which takes place between women who are and want to continue to be different but at the same time are united in the struggle for equal rights for all women. Elisabeth Beck-Gernsheim argues how dialogic feminism and its inclusion of the "other women" takes migrant women into account.

Judith Butler is the most cited author in feminist literature. Her book *Gender Trouble* opened key reflections on queer theory and in gender studies in general. Like any relevant innovation, that work gave rise to a great deal of controversy and reactions, to which she responded in her later work *Bodies That Matter.* In the book *Antigone's Claim*, she rethinks, from a woman's perspective, some of the reference points of our culture that have remained up to now untouchable. In the first chapter of this book, titled "The Question of Social Transformation," Butler makes a revision of *Gender Trouble* with contributions that extend and at times rectify its contents, reflecting upon the political task of feminist theory and considering the dual nature of norms. Her defense of human rights is especially gratifying for those of us who situate ourselves in dialogic feminism.

Lídia Puigvert is an author who has had international repercussions with her contributions about opening feminism to the plurality of voices of all women, and especially to the vast majority without university studies. This is a topic that she deals with in the second chapter, "Dialogic Feminism." This contribution has been received with particular enthusiasm among the movements of "other"—nonacademic—women, from which Puigvert asserts she has learned all that she writes about now. She has also raised a range of different responses among those of us who until now have substituted for the voices of these women. Almost all of us have witnessed with excitement how a feminist from a younger generation—with an internationally recognized scientific reputation as well as egalitarian goals—has surpassed what we feminists of the eighties and nineties did.

Elisabeth Beck-Gernsheim is co-author of *The Normal Chaos of Love* and is one of the main international references on key issues such as the social repercussions of research on the human genome. In the third chapter, "Migrant Women, Domestic Work, and Marriage," Beck includes in her conception of dialogic feminism the issue of women who are compelled to emigrate to other countries to better their lot, either by seeking work or by accepting offers of marriage from foreign men. The chronically failed distribution of domestic labor between women and men in privileged countries has often led to the transference of this work to women who come from poorer countries and who, frequently, do not enjoy decent labor conditions. All of them are women whose voices have been supplanted.

In the fourth chapter, "Transformative Encounters," Butler points out shared themes of both herself and Puigvert: feminist theory and the task of social transformation, the politics of inclusion, radical democracy, and inclusive social movements. She responds to Puigvert's text by focusing part of her analysis on the need for recognition of "the other" in order to reach transformation. Her reflections about dialogue contribute to the development of dialogic feminism. In the fifth chapter, "Equality of Differences," Puigvert also addresses themes that are close to them both, such as universal values, human rights, and a disassociation from postmodern positions, and she develops these themes by taking into account the contributions of Butler's text. She insists on the need for egalitarian dialogue as key to the reformulation of gender relations, and she makes this proposal from the dialogue that she herself maintains with the "other women."

This book is a result of a conference on Women and Social Transformation held in Barcelona, Spain, in 2001. Chapters 6 and 7 are transcripts of dialogues and a press interview from that conference.

Rosa Valls
University of Barcelona

The Question
of Social Transformation

It was a jarring moment, the moment in which I received this invitation. Would I have to write some essays making plain the relationship of my view of feminist theory to the question of social transformation? In a way, the very question caught me by surprise, since how could it be that anything called "feminist" could not in advance have an inherent relationship to social transformation? After all, feminism is about the social transformation of gender relations, and we could probably all agree on that, even if "gender" is not the preferred word for some. And yet, the question that is posed to me and my colleagues is what this relationship is. And so we are asked to make clear what we already assume but which is not at all to be taken for granted. Among us, we may imagine social transformation differently. We may have our own ideas of the world as it would be, or should be, transformed by feminism. We may have very different ideas of what social transformation is, or what qualifies as a transformative exercise. But we must also have an idea of how theory relates to the process of transformation: whether theory is itself a transformative task or whether it has transformation as one of its effects.

In what follows, I will argue that theory is itself transformative, so I will state that in advance. But you must also understand that I do not think theory is sufficient for social and political transformation. Something besides theorizing must take place: interventions at social and political levels which involve actions, sustained labor, and institutionalized practice, which are not quite the same as the exercise of theory. But I would also add that in all of these practices, theory is presupposed. In the very act of social transformation, we are all lay philosophers, presupposing a vision of the world, of what is right, of what is just, of what is abhorrent, of what human action is and can be, of what constitutes the necessary and sufficient conditions of life.

There are many questions that form the various foci of feminist research, and I would not want to identify any one of them as the essential or defining one. I would say, however, that the question of life is in some ways at the center of much feminist theory and, in particular, feminist philosophy. The question might be posed in various ways: What is the good life? How has the good life been conceived such that women's lives have not been included in its conceptualization? What would the good life be for women? But perhaps there is, prior to these questions, all of which are important, another one: the question of survival itself. And when we consider what feminist thought might be in relation to survival, a different set of questions emerge: Whose life is counted as a life? Whose prerogative is it to live? How do we decide when life begins and ends, and how do we weigh one life against another? Under what conditions should life come into being, and through what means? Who cares for life as it emerges, and who tends to the life of the child? Who cares for the life of the mother, and of what value is that life ultimately? And to what extent does gender—coherent gender—secure a life as livable? What threat of death is delivered to those who do not live gender according to its accepted norms?

That questions of life and death have always figured in feminist thought means that feminism has always, to some extent and in some way, been philosophical. That it asks how we organize life, how we accord it value, how we safeguard it against violence, how we compel the world and its institutions to inhabit new values means that its philosophical pursuits are in some sense at one with the aim of social transformation.

It would be easier if I could lay out for you what I think the ideal relation between genders should be, how gender should be experienced, in what equality and justice in relation to gender would consist. You would then know the norms that guide my thinking, and you could judge whether or not I have achieved the aims that I have set for myself. But I will not be that easy to read. And my difficulty will emerge not out of stubbornness or a will to be obscure. It will emerge simply out of the double truth that although we need norms in order to live, and to live well, to know in what direction to transform our social world, we are also constrained by norms in ways that sometimes do violence to us and that, for reasons of social justice, we must oppose. There is perhaps a confusion here, since many will say that the opposition to violence must take place *in the name of the norm*, i.e., a norm of nonviolence and respect, a norm that governs or compels respect for life itself. But consider that normativity has this double meaning. On the one hand, it refers to the aims and aspirations that guide us, the precepts by which we are compelled to act or speak to one another, the commonly held presuppositions by which we are oriented and which give direction to our actions. On the other hand, normativity refers to the process of normalization, the way that certain norms, ideas, and ideals hold sway over embodied life and provide coercive criteria for normal "men" and "women." And in this second sense, we see that norms are what govern "intelligible" life, "real" men and "real" women, and that when we defy these norms, it is unclear whether we are still living, or ought to be; whether our lives are valuable, or can be made to be; whether our genders are real, or can ever be regarded as such.

Now, a good Enlightenment thinker will simply shake her head and say that if one objects to normalization, it is in the name of a different norm. But that critic would also have to consider what the relationship is between normalization and normativity. It may be that when we talk about what binds us together as humans—what forms of speech or thinking we seek recourse to in an effort to find a common bond—we are, inevitably, seeking recourse to socially instituted relations, ones that have been formed over time and which give us a sense of the "common" only by excluding those lives that do not fit the norm. In this sense, we see the "norm" as that which binds us together, but we also see that the norm creates unity only through a strategy of exclusion. It will be necessary for us to think through this problem of the double nature of norms. But in this essay, I start by asking about the kind of norms that govern gender, and to ask in particular how they constrain and enable life, how they designate in advance what will and will not be a livable existence. I proceed with this first task through a review of *Gender Trouble*, the text through which I originally offered my theory of gender.[1] I consider this theory of gender explicitly in terms of the questions of violence, and the possible transformation of the scene of gender violence into a future of social survival. Secondly, I consider this double nature of the norms, showing how we cannot do without them, and how we do not have to assume that their form is given or fixed. Indeed, even if we cannot do without them, it will be seen that we also cannot accept them as they are. I pursue this paradox toward the end of my remarks in order to elucidate what I take to be the political stakes of feminist theory.

Reflections on Gender Trouble

When I wrote *Gender Trouble,* I was eleven years younger than I am today, and I was without a job. I wrote it for a few friends of mine, and I imagined maybe one or two hundred people might read it. I had two aims at the time: The first was to expose what I took to be a pervasive heterosexism in feminist theory; the second was to try to imagine a world in which those who live at some distance from gender norms, who live in the confusion of gender norms, might still understand themselves not only as living livable lives, but as deserving of a certain kind of recognition. But let us be more honest than that. I wanted *Gender Trouble* not only to be understood and accorded dignity, according to some humanist ideal, but to disturb—fundamentally—the way in which feminist and social theory think of gender, to make it exciting to understand something of the desire that gender trouble is, the desire it solicits, the desire it conveys.

So let me consider these two points again, since they have both changed in my mind and, as a result, compel me to rethink the question of change.

In the first instance, feminist theory. What did I understand its heterosexism to be then, and how do I understand it now? At the time, I understood the theory of sexual difference to be a theory of heterosexuality. And I also understood French feminism, with the exception of Monique Wittig, as perceiving cultural intelligibility not only in terms of assuming the fundamental difference between masculine and feminine, but of reproducing it. The theory was derived from Lévi-Strauss, Lacan, and Saussure, and there were various breaks with those masters which one could trace. Julia Kristeva said that Lacan made no room for the semiotic, and she insisted on offering that domain not only as a supplement to the symbolic, but as a way of undoing it. It was Hélène Cixous who saw feminine writing as a way of making the sign travel in ways that Lévi-Strauss could not imagine at the end of *The Elementary Structures of Kinship*. And Irigaray imagined the "goods [women as male-perceived commodities] getting together," and even implicitly theorized a certain kind of homoerotic love between women when those lips were all entangled and you couldn't tell the difference between the one and the other (and where not being able to tell the difference was not equivalent to "being the same"). The high at the time was to see that these French feminists had entered into a region considered fundamental to language and culture, an assertion that language came into being through sexual difference; that the speaking subject was one who emerged in relation to the duality of the sexes; that culture, as outlined by Lévi-Strauss, was defined through the exchange of women; and that the difference between men and women was instituted at the level of elementary exchange, an exchange which forms the possibility of communication itself.

To understand the exhilaration of this theory for those who were working within it, and for those who still do, one has to understand the sea change which took place when feminist studies went from being the analysis of "images" of women in this or that discipline or sphere of life to being an analysis of sexual difference at the foundation of cultural and human communicability. Suddenly, we were fundamental. Suddenly, no human science could proceed without us.

And not only were we fundamental, but we were changing that foundation. There was a new writing, a new form of communicability, a challenge to the kinds of communicability which were fully constrained by a patriarchal symbolic. And there were also new ways for women as "goods" to get together: new, poetic modes of alliance and cultural production. We had as it were the outlines of the theory of patriarchy before us, and we were also intervening in it, to produce new forms of intimacy, alliance, and communicability which were outside of its terms, but were also contesting its inevitability, its totalizing claim.

All well and good, but it did produce some problems for many of us. In the first place, it seemed that the model of culture, in both its patriarchal and feminist modes, assumed that there was a constancy of sexual difference; but there were those of us for whom gender trouble was the contestation of sexual difference

itself. There were many who asked whether they were women—
some asked it in order to become included in the category, and
some asked it in order to find out whether there were alternatives to being in the category. Denise Riley wrote that she did
not want to be exhausted by the category[2] but Cherrie Moraga
and others were also beginning to theorize butch-femme categories, which called into question whether the kinds of masculin-
ities at stake for a butch were always determined by an already
operative sexual difference, or whether they were calling sexual
difference into question.[3] And for a femme as well, was this a
femininity defined in relation to a masculinity already operative
in the culture, part of a normative structure which could not be
changed, or was this the challenge to that normative structure, a
challenge from within its most cherished terms? What happens
when terms such as *butch* and *femme* emerge not as simple copies of heterosexual masculinity and heterosexual femininity,
but as expropriations that expose the nonnecessary status of
their assumed meanings? Indeed, the point that *Gender Trouble*
made, and it is the point that is most widely cited (and will probably be on my tombstone one day) was that categories like butch
and femme are not copies of a more originary heterosexuality,
but show how the so-called originals—men and women within
the heterosexual framework—are similarly constructed and performatively established. So the ostensible copy is not explained
through reference to an origin, but the origin is understood to be
as performative as the copy. Through performativity, dominant
and nondominant gender norms are equalized. But some of
those performative accomplishments claim the place of nature
or of symbolic necessity, and they do this only by occluding the
ways in which they are performatively established.

⚉

I'll return to the theory of performativity in a moment, but for
now, let me explain how my account of this particular rift
between high structuralist feminist theory and poststructuralist
gender trouble has become reformulated for me.

In the first instance, you can see at work in my exposition of this
transition—the transition, one might say, from sexual difference to
gender trouble, or indeed, from sexual difference to queer theory—
that there is a slippage between sexual difference as a category

which conditions the emergence into language and culture, and gender as a sociological concept figured as a norm. Sexual difference is not the same as the categories of "women" and "men." Women and men exist, we might say, as social norms, and they are, I think, ways in which sexual difference has assumed content. Many Lacanians, for instance, argued with me that sexual difference has only a formal character, that nothing follows from the concept of sexual difference about the social roles or meanings that gender might have. Indeed, some of them evacuate sexual difference of every possible semantic meaning, allying it with the structural possibility for semantics, but leaving it no proper or necessary semantic content. Indeed, they even argue that the possibility of critique emerges when one comes to understand not only how sexual difference has become concretized in certain cultural and social instances, but how it has become reduced to its instance, which constitutes a fundamental mistake, a way of foreclosing the fundamental openness of the distinction itself.

So this is one way of answering me, and it comes from the formalist Lacanians, such as Joan Copjec, Charles Shepherdson, and also Slavoj Žižek. But there is a stronger feminist argument that implicitly or explicitly takes issue with the trajectory I have laid out. And it is articulated perhaps most buoyantly and persuasively by Rosi Braidotti.[4] I think the argument goes something like this: We must maintain the framework of sexual difference because it brings to the fore the continuing cultural and political reality of patriarchal domination, because it reminds us that whatever permutations of gender there may be, they do not fully challenge the framework within which they take place, for that framework persists at a symbolic level which is difficult to intervene upon. Critics such as Carol Anne Tyler argue, for instance, that it will always be different for a woman to enter into transgressive gender norms than it will be for a man, and that *Gender Trouble* does not distinguish strongly enough between these very different positions of power within society.

Others suggest that the problem has to do with psychoanalysis and with the place and meaning of Oedipalization; the child enters desire through triangulation, and whether or not there is a heterosexual pair who are functioning as the parents, the child will still locate a paternal and a maternal point of departure, and this will have symbolic significance for the child and become the structure through which desire is given form.

In a sense, there are important alternatives to be thought about together here. And I do not say that they should be reconciled. It may be that they stand in a necessary tension to one another—a necessary tension which now structures the field of feminist and queer theory—which, we might say, is an inevitable tension, but which necessitates their dialogue as well. It is important to distinguish between theorists of sexual difference who argue on biological grounds that the distinction between the sexes is necessary (the German feminist Barbara Duden tends to do this[5]) and those who argue that sexual difference is a fundamental nexus through which language and culture emerge (as do the structuralists and non-gender-troubled poststructuralists). But then there is a further distinction: There are those who find the structuralist paradigm useful only because it charts the continuing power differential between men and women in society and gives us a way of understanding how deeply it functions in establishing the symbolic order in which we live. Among these last, I think, there is a difference still between those who consider this symbolic order inevitable, and thus ratify patriarchy as an inevitable structure of culture, and those who think that sexual difference is inevitable and fundamental but that its form as patriarchal is contestable. Rosi Braidotti belongs to this last, and you can see why it would be most probably her with whom I have had useful conversations.

So it is when we try to understand whether sexual difference is necessarily heterosexist. Is it? Again, it depends on which version you accept: You can claim that Oedipalization presupposes heterosexual parenting or a heterosexual symbolic that supersedes whatever parenting arrangement is at work, if any; or you can hold that Oedipalization produces heterosexual desire and that sexual difference is a function of Oedipalization—in either case, it seems that the matter is closed. And there are those, such as Juliet Mitchell, who continue to be troubled by the question. If you recall, she is the one who, in *Psychoanalysis and Feminism*, declared the patriarchal symbolic order not to be a changeable set of rules but "primordial law."[6]

I take the point that the sociological concepts of gender, women, and men cannot be reducible to sexual difference. But I worry still about how to understand sexual difference as the operation of a symbolic order. What does it mean for such an order to be symbolic rather than social? And what happens to the social-transformation task of feminist theory if we accept that sexual difference is orchestrated and constrained at a symbolic level? If it is symbolic, is it changeable? I ask Lacanians this question and they tell me that changes in the symbolic take a long, long time. I wonder how long I will have to wait. Or they show me a few passages in what is called the Rome Discourse, and I wonder if these passages are the ones to which we are supposed to cling. And is it really true that sexual difference at the symbolic level is without semantic content? Can it ever be? And what if we have indeed done nothing more than abstracted the social meaning of sexual difference and exalted it as a symbolic and hence presocial structure? Is that a way of making sure that sexual difference is beyond contestation?

You might wonder after all of this why I want to contest sexual difference at all, so let me remind you: *Gender Trouble* starts with the assumption that gender is complexly produced through identificatory and performative practices, and that gender is not as clear or as univocal as we are sometimes led to believe. I wanted to combat forms of essentialism which claimed that gender is a truth that is somehow there as a given, undeniable and interior to the body, as a natural core. On the other hand, the theory of sexual difference makes none of the claims that natural essentialism does. These were the two different kinds of challenges that *Gender Trouble* needed to meet. I see now that I needed to separate the issues and I hope that I have begun to do that in my subsequent work. But I still worry that the frameworks we commit ourselves to, because they describe patriarchal domination, may well recommit us to seeing that very domination as inevitable. Is the symbolic eligible for social intervention? Does sexual difference really remain Other to its instituted form, the dominant one being heterosexuality itself? Let me turn now to the question of what it was that I imagined, and what I now imagine, and how the process of change, and the question of politics, has changed.

Gender Trouble ends with a discussion of drag, and the final chapter is in fact called "From Parody to Politics." A number of critics have scrutinized that chapter in order to find wherein lies the transition: How do we get from parody to politics? There are those who think that the text belittles politics, reducing it to parody, while others claim that drag becomes a model for resistance or for political intervention and participation more generally. So let us reconsider this controversial closing, a text I probably wrote too quickly and whose future I did not anticipate at the time.

Why drag? Well, there are biographical reasons, and you might as well know that the only way to describe me in my younger years was as a bar dyke who spent her days reading Hegel and her evenings, well, at the gay bar, which occasionally became a drag bar. So there I was, undergoing a cultural moment in the midst of a social and political struggle. But I also experienced in that moment a certain implicit theorization of gender: It quickly dawned on me that some of these so-called men could do the feminine turn much better than I ever could, ever wanted to, ever would. And so I was confronted by what can only be called the transferability of the attribute. Femininity, which I understood never to have belonged to me anyway, clearly lay elsewhere, and I have always been much happier being the audience to it than I could ever be as an embodiment of it. Indeed, whether we follow the framework of sexual difference or of gender trouble, I would hope that we would all remain committed to the ideal that no one should be forcibly compelled to occupy a gender norm that is experienced by that person as a violation. And it is a violation, one that not only is there in the culture, as an interpellation that you refuse only by accepting the consequences—which can be your life—but also as a set of laws, as criminal and psychiatric codes for which imprisonment or institutionalization are still possible options. Gender dysphoria can still be used in many countries to deny you a job or to take away your child. The consequences can be severe. It won't do to call this "play" or "fun." And I don't mean to say it is not sometimes play, pleasure, fun, fantasy. I mean to say only that we continue to live in a world in which you can risk serious disenfranchisement and physical violence for the pleasure you seek, the fantasy you embody, the gender you perform.

For the most part, I am known for the discussion that takes place in about eight paragraphs of *Gender Trouble,* i.e., those on drag performances and their subversive potential. I have been criticized for reducing politics to drag performances and for thinking that all drag performances are somehow subversive. I have been asked, subversive of what? And is there more to politics and to gender than drag? I would like to take a moment to clarify this view, and to clarify, in particular, how my current thinking on this issue has changed. Let me begin by offering a few propositions to consider:

(A) What operates at the level of cultural fantasy is not finally dissociable from the ways in which material life is organized.

(B) When one performance of gender is considered real and another false, or when one presentation of gender is considered authentic and another fake, then we can conclude that a certain ontology of gender is conditioning these judgments, one that is also put into crisis by the performance of gender in such a way that these judgments are not easily made or become impossible to make.

(C) The point to emphasize here is not that drag is subversive of gender norms, but that we live with received notions of reality and accounts of ontology which are implicit and determine what kinds of bodies and sexualities will be considered real and true, and what kinds will not.

(D) This differential effect of ontological presuppositions on the embodied life of individuals has consequential effects. And what drag can point out is that (1) this set of ontological presuppositions is at work and (2) it is open to rearticulation.

The question of who and what is considered real and true is apparently a question of knowledge. But it is also, as Foucault makes plain, a question of power. Having or bearing "truth" and "reality" is an enormously powerful prerogative within the social world—one way in which power dissimulates as ontology. According to Foucault, one of the first tasks of critique is to discern the relation "between mechanisms of coercion and elements of knowledge."[7] Here we are confronted with the limits of what is knowable, limits which exercise a certain force but are not grounded in any necessity, limits which one interrogates only at a risk to one's secure and available ontology: "[N]othing can exist as an element of knowledge if, on the one hand, it . . . does not conform to a set of rules and constraints characteristic, for example, of a given type of scientific discourse in a given period, and if, on the other hand, it does not possess the effects of coercion or simply the incentives peculiar to what is scientifically validated or simply rational or simply generally accepted, etc." (52). Knowledge and power are not finally separable, but work together to establish a set of subtle and explicit criteria for thinking about the world: "It is therefore not a matter of describing what knowledge is and what power is and how one would repress the other or how the other would abuse the one, but rather, a nexus of knowledge-power has to be described so that we can grasp what constitutes the acceptability of a system" (52–53).

If we consider this relation of knowledge and power in relation to gender, it seems we are compelled to ask how gender is organized such that it comes to function as a presupposition about how the world is structured. So, there is no merely epistemological approach to gender, no simple way to ask, what are women's ways of knowing? or what might it mean to know women? On the contrary, the ways in which women are said to "know" or to "be known" are already orchestrated by power precisely at that moment in which the terms of "acceptable" categorization are instituted.

In Foucault's view, the critic thus has a double task: to show how knowledge and power work to constitute a more or less systematic way of ordering the world with its own "conditions of acceptability of a system," but also "to follow the breaking points which indicate its emergence." So it will not be enough to isolate and identify the peculiar nexus of power and knowledge that gives rise to the field of intelligible things, but one must also track the way in which that field meets its breaking point, the moments of its discontinuities, the sites where it fails to constitute the intelligibility it promises. What this means is that one looks for both the conditions by which the object field is constituted and the limits of those conditions, the moment at which they point up their contingency and their transformability. In Foucault's terms, "schematically speaking, we have perpetual mobility, essential fragility or rather the complex interplay between what replicates the same process and what transforms it" (58).

What this means for gender, then, is that it is important not only to understand how the terms of gender are instituted, naturalized, established as presuppositional, but to trace the moments at which the binary system of gender is disputed and challenged, where the coherence of the categories are put into question, where the very social life of gender turns out to be malleable and transformable.

The turn to drag performance was, in part, a way to think about not only how gender is performed, but how it is resignified, and what the collective terms are by which its resignification can and does take place. Drag performers, for instance, tend to live in communities, and there are strong ritual bonds, such as those we see in the film *Paris Is Burning*, which make us aware of the resignification of social bonds that gender minorities can forge. Thus, we are talking about a cultural life of fantasy that not only organizes the material conditions of life, but also produces sustaining bonds of community, which offers recognition and works to ward off violence, racism, homophobia, transphobia. We see this threat of violence, and it tells us something about what is fundamental to the culture in which they live, a culture which is not radically distinct from the one in which many of us live, a culture which is not one, singular, even though it is not the same as that in which any of us probably live. But there is a reason we understand it, if we do; there is a reason that *Paris Is Burning* has achieved notoriety in mainstream channels—because its beauty, its tragedy, its pathos, its bravery, its pleasure has a way of crossing cultural boundaries; because what also crosses those boundaries, and not always in the same way, is the threat of violence, the threat of poverty, the struggle to survive. And here it is important to note that the struggle to survive is not really separable from the cultural life of fantasy. It is part of it. Fantasy is what allows us to imagine ourselves and others otherwise. Fantasy is what establishes the possible in excess of the real; it points elsewhere, and when it is embodied, it brings the elsewhere home. And this brings me back to the question of politics. How is it that drag or, indeed, much more than drag, transgender itself, enters into the political field? It does this, I would suggest, by not only making us question what is real, and what has to be, but by so doing, showing us how contemporary notions of reality can be questioned and new modes of reality instituted. And it shows that we can do this in our very embodiment and as a consequence of being a body that is in the mode of becoming. In becoming otherwise, it exceeds the norm, reworks the norm, and makes us see how realities to which we thought we were confined are not written in stone. We should not underestimate what the thought of the possible does for those who have survival as a burning question.

So this is one way in which the matter is and continues to be political. But there is something more, since what the example of drag sought to do was to make us question the means by which reality is made, and to consider the way in which being called "real" or "not real" can be not only a means of social control, but dehumanizing violence. Indeed, I would put it this way: To be called not real, and to have that label institutionalized as a form of differential treatment is to become the Other against which the human is measured. It is the unhuman, the beyond the human, the less than human, the other side of the border which secures the human in its ostensible reality. To be called a copy, to be called not real, is thus one way in which one can be oppressed. But consider that it is more fundamental than that. For, to be oppressed means that you already exist as a subject of some kind, you are there as the visible and oppressed Other for the master subject, as a possible or potential subject. But to be not real is something else again. To be oppressed you must at least be intelligible. To find that you are fundamentally unintelligible (indeed, that the laws of culture and of language find you to be an impossibility) is to have not yet achieved access to the human, to find yourself speaking but that your language is hollow, as if you were human but with the sense that you are not, to find that no recognition is forthcoming because the norms by which recognition takes place are not in your favor.

If gender is performative, then it follows that reality is itself produced as an effect of the performance, that although there are norms which govern what will and will not be real, what will and will not be intelligible, they are called into question and re-iterated at the moment in which performativity begins its citational practice. One surely cites norms that already exist, but these norms can be significantly deterritorialized through the citation. And they can be exposed as nonnatural and nonnecessary when they take place in a context and through an embodying that defies normative expectation. What this means is that through the practice of gender performativity, we not only see how the norms that govern reality are cited, but we also see one of the mechanisms by which reality is reproduced and altered in the course of that reproduction. The point of drag is not simply to produce a pleasurable and subversive spectacle, but to allegorize the spectacular and consequential ways in which reality is both reproduced and contested. And this has consequences for how gender presentations are criminalized and pathologized, how subjects who cross gender risk imprisonment and institutionalization, why violence against transgendered subjects is not recognized as violence, why it is sometimes inflicted by the very states which should be offering such subjects protection from violence.

I take this to be essential to politics, and, in ending this section, I will try to say why. I am sometimes asked the following question: So what if new forms of gender are possible; how does this affect the ways that we live, the concrete needs of the human community? And how are we to distinguish between forms of gender possibility which are valuable and those which are not? First, I would say that it is not a question merely of producing a new future for genders which do not yet exist. The genders I have in mind have existed for a long time, but they have not been admitted into the terms which govern reality. So it is a question of developing, within law, within psychiatry, within social and literary theory, a new legitimating lexicon for the gender complexity we have always been living. Because the norms governing reality have not admitted these forms to be real, we will, of necessity, call them new. But I hope we will laugh knowingly when and if we do. And if we think that this is a theory of mere indulgence, then consider that the necessary background for gender trouble is the question of survival, the question of how to create a world in which those who understand their gender and their desire to be nonnormative can live and thrive not only without the threat of violence from the outside, but without the pervasive sense of their own unreality, which can and has led to suicide, i.e., self-destructiveness and literal suicide. Lastly, I would ask what place the thinking of the possible has within political theorizing. One can object and say, ah, but you are trying only to make gender complexity possible, but that does not tell us which forms are good or bad—it does not supply the measure, the gauge, the norm. And that is right. It does not supply the measure, the gauge, the norm. But there is a normative aspiration here, and it has to do with the ability to live and breathe and move, and would no doubt belong somewhere in what is called a philosophy of freedom. The thought of a possible life is an indulgence only for those who already know themselves to be possible. For those who are still looking to become possible, possibility is a necessity.

Let me offer a story here, before moving on to consider the

double character of norms. As you probably know, there is a new and important movement of individuals who are opposing corrective genital surgery of infants. Approximately 2–3% of infants in the world population per year are born with genitals which are not readily identifiable as male or female. They may be mixed; they may be indeterminate. A recent case highlights the social vulnerability that intersexed people endure. In a heavily publicized case in the United States, a young boy who lost his penis in a botched surgery was raised as a girl and lived uneasily with his feminine gender for most of his early years. At school, he still had the impulse to stand while urinating, even though he did not have a penis, and in the bathrooms, the girls, who noticed this, threatened to kill him if he continued to do that. We have to wonder about this threat of violence. Where does it come from? What is so terrible for those who see this act that they are inspired to threaten violence and death? What is its purpose? And how might it be transformed?

The desire to kill someone for not conforming to the gender norm by which he or she is "supposed" to live suggests that life itself requires this norm, and that to be and live outside it is to court death. The person who threatens this violence emerges from the anxious and rigid belief that a sense of world and of self will be radically undermined if such a being, uncategorizable, is permitted to live within the social world. The negation, through violence, of that body is a vain effort to restore order, to renew the social world on the basis of intelligible gender, and to refuse the challenge to rethink that world as something other than natural or necessary. This is not far removed from the threat of death or murder of transsexuals in various countries, and of gay men who read "feminine" or gay women who read "masculine." I can give you many graphic examples, and they are widespread— sometimes countered by police, sometimes aided and abetted by police;[8] sometimes denounced by governments and international agencies, sometimes not included as legible or "real" crimes against humanity by those very institutions.

But if we oppose this violence, then we do so in the name of what? What is the alternative to this violence? And for what transformation of the social world do I call if we understand this violence to emerge from a profound desire to keep the order of binary gender natural or necessary, to make of it a structure, either natural, cultural, or both, which no "human" can oppose and still remain human? If someone opposes these norms, not just by having a point of view about them, but incorporating this opposition into the body and a corporeal style which is legible, then it seems that violence emerges precisely as the demand to counter that opposition. But this is not a simple difference in points of view. To counter that opposition by violence is to say, effectively, that this body, this challenge, to an accepted version of the world is and shall be unthinkable. It is an effort to expunge what renders the gendered order of intelligibility contingent, frail, and open to fundamental transformation.

So the ethical task that emerges in light of such an analysis is: How might we encounter the difference that calls our grids of intelligibility into question without trying to kill or foreclose the challenge that the difference delivers? What might it mean to learn to live in the anxiety of that challenge, to feel the surety of one's epistemological and ontological anchor go, but to be willing, in the name of the human, to allow the human to become something other than what it is traditionally assumed to be? This means that we must learn to live, and to embrace, the destruction and rearticulation of the human in the name of a more capacious and, finally, less violent world, not to know in advance what precise form our humanness will take, but to be open to its permutations, in the name of nonviolence. Emmanuel Levinas has taught us, wisely, that the question to be posed is simple but unanswerable: "Who are you?"⁹ The violent response to the Other knows that it does not know, and does not want to not know. It wants to shore up what it takes for granted and expunge what threatens it with not knowing, what forces it to reconsider the presuppositions of its world and their contingency and malleability. The nonviolent response lives with its not knowing in the face of the Other, since sustaining the bond which the question opens to is finally more valuable than having a surety in advance about what defines the human and what its future life will most likely be.

Norms and Normativity: A Double Bind

Normativity sometimes does mean social norms, or more particularly, the normalizing effects of social norms, as is the focus of cultural theory (e.g., that of Michael Warner and Lauren Berlant).

For Habermasians, it carries a quite different valence, signifying the domain of justificatory practices and referring always to the question of grounding. I very much accept the thesis of François Ewald that social norms are not reducible to law or, indeed, to Law (in a Lacanian sense).

For Ewald, norms emerge as part of the sociological effort to approximate averages, to calculate what most people do under so-called normal circumstances. They are implicit ideals or notions which inform common practices of normalcy. Ewald makes clear that a norm is not the same as a rule or a law.[10] A norm operates within social practices as the implicit standard of normalization. Although a norm may be analytically separable from the practices in which it is embedded, it may prove to be recalcitrant to any effort to decontextualize its operation. Norms may or may not be explicit, and when they operate as the normalizing principle in social practice, they usually remain implicit, difficult to read, discernible most clearly and dramatically in the effects that they produce.

For gender to be a norm suggests that it is always and only tenuously embodied by any particular social actor. The norm governs the social intelligibility of action, but it is not the same as the action that it governs. The norm appears to be indifferent to the actions that it governs, by which I mean only that the norm appears to have a status and effect that is independent of the actions governed by the norm. The norm governs intelligibility and allows for certain kinds of practices and action to become recognizable, imposing a grid of legibility onto the social and defining the parameters of what will and will not appear within its domain. The question of what it is to be outside the norm poses a paradox, for if the norm renders the social field intelligible, i.e., normalizes that field for us, then to be outside the norm is in some sense to still be defined in relation to it: To be not quite masculine or not quite feminine is still to be understood exclusively in terms of one's relationship to the quite masculine and the quite feminine.

To claim that gender is a norm is not quite the same as saying that there are normative views of femininity and masculinity, even though there clearly are such normative views. Gender is not exactly what one "is," nor is it precisely what one "has." Gender is the apparatus by which the production and normalization of masculine and feminine take place along with the interstitial forms of hormonal, chromosomal, psychic, and performative embodiment which gender assumes. To assume that gender always and exclusively means "the matrix of the 'masculine' and 'feminine'" is precisely to miss the critical point that the production of that coherent binary is contingent, that it comes at a cost, and that those permutations of gender that do not fit the binary are as much a part of gender as its most normative instance. To conflate the definition of gender with its normative expression is inadvertently to reconsolidate the power of the norm to constrain the definition of gender. Gender is the mechanism by which notions of masculine and feminine are produced and naturalized, but gender might very well be the apparatus by which such terms are deconstructed and denaturalized. Indeed, it may be that the very apparatus that seeks to install the norm also works to undermine that very installation, that the installation is, as it were, definitionally incomplete. To keep the term "gender" apart from both masculinity and femininity is to safeguard a theoretical perspective by which one might offer an account of how the binary of masculine and feminine comes to exhaust the semantic field of gender. Whether one refers to "gender trouble" or "gender blending," "transgender" or "cross-gender," one is already suggesting that gender has a way of moving beyond that naturalized binary. The conflation of gender with masculine/feminine, man/woman, male/female thus performs the very naturalization that the notion of gender is meant to forestall.

Thus, a restrictive discourse on gender that insists on the binary of "man" and "woman" as the exclusive way to understand the gender field performs a regulatory operation of power, naturalizing the hegemonic instance, foreclosing the thinkability of its disruption.

For Ewald, a norm operates as an ideal point; indeed, as an elaboration of what Foucault, in the first volume of *The History of Sexuality*, termed "a regulatory ideal."[11] It is the point of reference, implicit, abstract, and speculative, by which human activity orients itself and which, in turn, supplies human activity with its sense of givenness and intelligibility. This sense of the norm is clearly quite different from what is meant by "normative" philosophy or, indeed, a "normative" account of social theory.

If we consider Habermas' argument in *Between Facts and Norms*, it is clear that he relies on norms to supply a common understanding for social actors and speakers: "Participants, in claiming validity for their utterances, strive to reach an understanding with one another about something in the world. . . . The everyday use of language does not turn exclusively or even primarily on its representational (or fact-stating) functions: here all the functions of language and language-world relations come into play, so that the spectrum of validity claims takes in more than truth claims."[12] He goes on to explain that "in explicating the meaning of linguistic expressions and the validity of statements, we touch on idealizations that are connected with the medium of language" (17). He makes clear that without these idealizations at the heart of language, we would not have the resources by which to orient ourselves to disparate kinds of claims made by any number of social actors. Indeed, the presumption of a common set of idealizations is what gives our action order, what orders it in advance, and what we take into account as we seek to order ourselves in relation to one another and a common future:

> With the concept of communicative action, which brings in mutual understanding as a mechanism of action coordination, the counterfactual presuppositions of actors who orient their action to validity claims also acquire *immediate relevance for the construction and preservation of social orders; for these orders* exist *through the recognition of normative validity claims.* (17, my emphasis)

Here we can see that norms, which orient action toward the common good and belong to an "ideal" sphere, are not precisely social in Ewald's sense. They do not belong to variable social orders, and they are not, in Foucault's sense, a set of "regulatory ideals" and, hence, part of the ideal life of social power. On the contrary, they function as part of a reasoning process which conditions any and every social order and gives that order its coherence. We know, though, that Habermas would not accept the "ordered" characteristic of any social order as a necessary good. Some orders clearly ought to be disrupted, and for good reason. Indeed, the order of gender intelligibility may well qualify as one such order. But do we have a way to distinguish here between the function of the norm as socially integrative and the value of "integration" under oppressive social conditions? In other words, is there not an inherently conservative function of the norm when it is said to preserve order? What if the very order is exclusionary or violent? We might respond, with Habermas, that violence goes against the normative idealizations functioning, implicitly, in everyday language. But if the norm is socially integrative, then how will it actually work to break up a social "order" purchased and maintained through violent means? Is the norm part of such a social order, or is it "social" only in a hypothetical sense, part of an "order" which is not instantiated in the social world as it is lived and negotiated?

⚬⚬⚬

If the Habermasian point is that we cannot hope to live in consensus or in common orientation without assuming such norms, my question is whether the "common" in this instance is not instituted precisely through the production of what is uncommon, what is outside the common, what disrupts it from within, what poses a challenge to its integrity. What is the value of the "common"? And do we need to know that, despite our differences, we are all oriented toward the same conception of rational deliberation and justification? Or do we need to know precisely that the "common" is no longer there for us, if it ever was, and that the capacious and self-limiting approach to difference is not only the task of cultural translation in this day of multiculturalism, but the most important way to nonviolence?

The point is not to apply social norms to lived social instances, to order and define them (as Foucault has criticized), nor is it to find justificatory mechanisms for the grounding of social norms that are extrasocial (even as they operate under the name of the "social"). There are times when both of these activities do and must take place: We level judgments against criminals for illegal acts and so subject them to a normalizing procedure; we consider our grounds for action in collective contexts and try to find modes of deliberation and reflection about which we can agree. But neither of these is all we do with norms. Through recourse to norms, the sphere of the humanly intelligible is circumscribed, and this circumscription is consequential for any ethics and any conception of social transformation. We might feel that we must know the fundamentals of the human in order to act in such a way that we preserve and promote human life as we know it. But what if the very categories of the human have excluded those who should be operating within its terms, who do not accept the modes of reasoning and justifying "validity claims" that have been proffered by Western forms of rationalism? Have we ever yet known the "human"? And what might it take to approach that knowing? Should we be wary of knowing it too soon or of any final or definitive knowing? If we take the field of the human for granted, then we fail to think critically—and ethically—about the consequential ways that the human is produced, reproduced, deproduced. This latter inquiry does not exhaust the field of ethics, but I cannot imagine a "responsible" ethics or theory of social transformation operating without it.

Let me suggest here by way of a closing discussion to this essay that the necessity of keeping our notion of the "human" open to a future articulation is essential to the project of international human rights discourse and politics. We see this time and again when the very notion of the human is presupposed; it is defined in advance, and in terms which are distinctively Western, very often American, and therefore parochial. The paradox emerges that the "human" at issue in human rights is already known, already defined, and yet is supposed to be the ground for a set of rights and obligations that are international. How we move from the local to the international is a major question for international politics, but it takes a specific form for international feminism. And I suggest that an anti-imperialist or at least nonimperialist conception of international human rights must call into question what is meant by human, and learn from the various ways and means by which it is defined across cultural venues. This means that local conceptions of what is human or, indeed, of what the basic conditions and needs of human life are must be subjected to reinterpretation, since there are historical and cultural circumstances in which "human" is defined differently, and its basic needs and, hence, basic entitlements are also defined differently.

I do not mean to offer a reductively relativist argument. I think that a reductive relativism would say that we cannot speak of the human or of international human rights, since there are only and always local and provisional understandings of these terms, and that the generalizations themselves do violence to the specificity of the meanings in question. This is not my view. We are compelled to speak of the human, and of the international, and to find out in particular how "human rights" do and do not work in favor of women, of what "women" are and what they are not. But to speak in this way, and to call for social transformations in the name of women, we must also be part of a critical democratic project, one which understands that the category of "human" has been used differentially and with exclusionary aims, that not all humans have been included within its terms, that the category of "women" has been used differentially and with exclusionary aims, and that not all women have been included within its terms, and that women have not been fully incorporated into the human, and that both categories are still in process, under way and unfulfilled. This means that we must follow a double path in politics: We must use this language, and use it to assert an entitlement to conditions of life in ways that are sensitive to the question of gender, and we must also subject our very categories to critical scrutiny, find out the limits of their inclusivity, the presuppositions they include, the ways in which they must be expanded to encompass the diversity of what it is to be human and gendered. When the UN conference at Beijing met a few years ago and we heard there a discourse on "women's human rights," the term struck many people as paradoxical. But think about what this term, coined by Charlotte Bunch, actually says. It says that the "human" is contingent, that it has in the past and continues in the present to define a variable and restricted population, which may or may not include women. It says that women have their own set of human rights, that what "human" comes to mean when we think about the humanness of women is perhaps different than what "human" has meant when it has functioned as presumptively male. It also says that these terms are defined variably, in relation to one another. And we could certainly make a similar argument about race. Which populations have qualified as the "human" and which have not? What is the history of this category? Where are we in its history at this time?

I would suggest that in this last process, we can rearticulate or resignify the basic categories of ontology—of being human, of being gendered—only to the extent that we submit ourselves to a process of cultural translation. And the point here is not to assimilate foreign or unfamiliar notions of gender or humanness into our own, as if it were simply a matter of incorporation. It is also a process of yielding our most fundamental categories, that is, of seeing how and why they yield to a rupture and a resignification when they encounter what is unknown, or not yet known. It is crucial to recognize that the notion of the "human" will be

built only over time in and by the process of a cultural translation that is not between two languages that stay self-enclosed,
distinct, unified. But rather, *translation will compel each language to change in order to apprehend the other,* and this appre-
hension, at the limit of what is familiar and parochial, will be the
occasion of both an ethical and a social transformation.

There are questions about the strategy of resignification as
politics. One might well say that politicians on either the right or
the left can use this strategy. And we can surely see how "multiculturalism" and "globalization" have their right-wing and left-
wing variants. In the United States, the word "compassionate"
has been recently linked to conservativism, which strikes many
of us as an abomination of resignification. One can point out,
with full justification, that National Socialism was a resignification of socialism. And that would be right. So it seems clear that
resignification alone is not sufficient as a descriptor of politics.
One can argue both that the Nazis appropriated power by turning
the language and concerns of democracy against democracy and
that the Haitian revolutionaries appropriated power by using the
terms of democracy against the slave-owning powers that would
deny it for blacks. And so the work of appropriation can be used
by either the right or the left, and there are no necessarily salu-
tary ethical consequences inherent to it. There is the queer appropriation of "queer," the rap/hip-hop appropriation of racist
discourse, the left-wing appropriation of an anti–big government
discourse, and on and on. Appropriation by itself leads to a my-
riad of consequences, some of which we might embrace and
some of which we might abhor.

But if resignification does work in the service of radical democratic politics, how might it work? I want to suggest here that as
we extend the realm of universality, becoming more knowing
about what justice implies and providing for greater possibilities
of "life"—which itself is a term contested by both reactionaries
and progressives—we need to assume that our already established conventions regarding what is human, what is universal,
what the meaning and substance of international politics might
be, are not sufficient. For the purposes of a radical democratic
transformation, we need to know that our fundamental categories can and must be expanded, to become more inclusive and
more responsive to the full range of cultural populations. This
does not mean that a social engineer plots at a distance how best

to include everyone in his or her category. It means that the category itself must be subjected to a multiple resignification, that it must emerge anew as a result of the cultural translations it undergoes.

What moves me politically is the moment in which a subject—a person, a collective—asserts a right or entitlement to a livable life when no such prior authorization exists, when no clearly enabling convention is in place. One might hesitate and say, but there are fascists who invoke rights for which there are no prior entitlements. It cannot be a good thing to invoke rights or entitlements to what one considers a "livable life" if that very life is based on racism or misogyny or violence or exclusion. And I would, of course, agree with this last. A better example to consider is when, prior to the overthrow of apartheid, some black South Africans arrived at the polling booths ready to vote. There was then, at that time, no prior authorization for their vote. They simply arrived. They performatively invoked the right to vote even when there was no prior authorization, no enabling convention in place. On the other hand, we might say that Hitler also invoked rights to a certain kind of life for which there was no constitutional or legal precedent, local or international. But there is a distinction between these two invocations, and it is crucial to my argument.

In both of these cases, the subjects in question invoked rights to which they were not entitled by existing law, though in both cases, existing law had international and local versions which were not fully compatible with one another. Those who opposed apartheid were not restricted to existing convention (although they were, clearly, invoking and citing international convention against local convention). The emergence of fascism in Germany, as well as that of constitutional government in postwar Germany, was also not limited to existing convention. These political phenomena involved innovation. But that does not answer the question of which action is right to pursue. Which innovation has value and which does not? *The norms that we would consult to answer this question cannot themselves be derived from resignification.* They have to be derived from a radical democratic theory and practice, and so resignification has to be contextualized in that way. One must make substantive decisions about what will lead to a less violent future and a more inclusive population, what will help to fulfill the claims of universality

and justice that we seek to understand in their cultural specificity and social meaning. It will then be crucial to ask: What forms
of community have been created, and through what violences
and exclusions? Hitler sought to intensify the violence of racism
and exclusion, while the anti-apartheid movement sought to
counter them. And that would be the basis on which I would
condemn the one and condone the other. The task of a radical
democratic theory and practice will thus be to ask what resources it must have in order to bring into the human community those humans who have not been considered part of the rec-
ognizably human, thus extending to previously disenfranchised
communities the norms that sustain viable life.

So I have concluded it seems with such a call to extend the
norms. Let me consider as a final gesture, then, the relation
between norms and life, since that has been crucial to my inquiry thus far. The question of life is a political one, although
perhaps not exclusively so. The question of the "right to life" has
affected the debates on the legalization of abortion. Feminists
who are in favor of abortion rights have been called "anti-life,"
and they have responded by asking, whose life? And when does
"life" begin? If you were to canvass feminists internationally on
the question of what life is or, perhaps more simply, when life begins, you would get many different views. And that is why, considered internationally, not all women's movements are united
on this question. There is the question of when "life" begins, and
then the question of when "human" life begins, or when the humanity of the human begins. Who knows? Who is equipped or
entitled to know? Whose knowledge holds sway and functions as
power here? Feminists have argued that the life of the mother
should be equally important as that of the fetus—then it is a
question of one life versus another. They have argued that every
child should be wanted and have a chance at a livable life, and
they have also argued that there are conditions for life that must
first be met: The mother must be well; there must be certainty
that the child will be well fed; and there must be some chance of
a future, of a viable and enduring future, since a human being
with no futurity loses its humanness and stands a chance of los-
ing its life as well. Here we see the term "life" functioning both
within feminism and between feminism and its opponents, as a
site of contest, an unsettled term, whose various meanings are
being proliferated and debated in different ways in the context of

different nation-states with different religious and philosophical conceptions. Indeed, some of my opponents may well argue that if one takes as a paramount value the "extension of norms that support viable life," it might follow, depending on your definitions, that the "unborn child" should be valued above all. This is not my view, and not my conclusion.

My argument against this conclusion has to do with the very use of "life," as if we know what it means, what it requires, what it demands. When we ask what makes a life livable, we are asking about certain normative conditions that must be fulfilled for life to become life. And so there are at least two senses of life: one which refers to the minimum biological form of living, and another which preexists to establish minimum conditions for a livable life.[13] And this implies not that we can disregard the former in favor of the latter, but that we must ask, as we did about gender violence, what humans require in order to maintain and reproduce the conditions of their own livability. And what are our politics such that we are, in whatever way is possible, both conceptualizing the possibility of the livable life and arranging for its institutional support?

There will always be disagreement about what this means, and those who claim that a single political direction is necessitated by virtue of this commitment will be mistaken. But this is only because to live is to live politically, in relation to power, in relation to others, in the act of assuming responsibility for a collective future. To assume responsibility for a future is not to know its direction fully in advance, since the future, especially the future with and for others, requires a certain openness and unknowingness. And it also implies that a certain agonism and contestation will and must be in play. It must be in play for politics to become democratic. Democracy does not speak in unison; its tunes are dissonant, and necessarily so. It is not a predictable process; it must be undergone, like a passion must be undergone. It may also be that life itself becomes foreclosed when the right way is decided in advance, when we impose what is right for everyone without finding a way to enter into community, and to discover there the "right" in the midst of cultural translation. It may be that what is "right" and what is "good" consist in staying open to the tensions that beset the most fundamental categories we require, to know unknowingness at the core of what we know, and what we need, and to recognize the sign of life—and its prospects—in the contestations which are ours to undergo with one another.

Notes

1. Judith Butler. 1990. *Gender Trouble: Feminism and the Subversion of Identity*. New York: Routledge.
2. Denise Riley. 1998. *"Am I That Name?" Feminism and the Category of "Women" in History*. Minneapolis: University of Minnesota Press.
3. Amber Moraga and Cherrie Hollibaugh. 1984. "What We're Rolling Around in Bed With." In: *Pleasure and Danger: Exploring Female Sexuality*. Ed. Carole S. Vance. Boston: Routledge and Kegan Paul.
4. See my interview with Rosi Braidotti. 1995. "Feminism by Any Other Name," in *Differences,* special issue on "More Gender Trouble: Feminism Meets Queer Theory," winter.
5. Barbara Duden. 1991. *The Woman Beneath the Skin: A Doctor's Patients in Eighteenth-Century Germany*. Cambridge, Mass: Harvard University Press.
6. Juliet Mitchell. 1974. *Psychoanalysis and Feminism*. New York: Pantheon, p. 370.
7. Michel Foucault. 1997. "What Is Critique?" In: *The Politics of Truth.* Ed. Sylvère Lotringer and Lysa Hochroth. New York: Semiotext(e). p. 50.
8. See announcements from the International Gay and Lesbian Human Rights Commission (IGLHRC): <http://www.iglhrc.org>
9. Adriana Cavarero. 2000. *Relating Narratives: Storytelling and Selfhood*. London: Routledge.
10. See François Ewald, "Norms, Discipline, and the Law," in *Law and the Order of Culture,* ed. Robert Post (Berkeley and Los Angeles: University of California Press, 1991): 138–161; "A Concept of Social Law," in *Dilemmas of Law in the Welfare State,* ed. Gunter Teubner (Walter de Gruyter, 1986): 40–71; "A Power Without an Exterior," in *Michel Foucault, Philosopher,* ed. Timothy Armstrong (New York: Routledge, 1992): 169–75; and Charles Taylor, "To Follow a Rule. . ." in *Bourdieu: Critical Perspectives,* ed. Craig Calhoun et al. (Chicago: University of Chicago Press, 1993): 45–60.
11. Michel Foucault. 1978. *The History of Sexuality,* vol. 1. New York: Pantheon, p. 155.
12. Jürgen Habermas. 1996. *Between Facts and Norms: Contributions to a Discourse Theory of Law and Democracy*. Cambridge, Mass: MIT Press, p. 16.
13. See Giorgio Agamben. 1998. *Homo Sacer: Sovereign Power and Bare Life*. Stanford, Cal: Stanford University Press.

Dialogic Feminism: "Other Women's" Contributions to the Social Transformation of Gender Relations

Introduction

Like many other academic women, I was first introduced to feminist literature when I began attending university. On March 8, 1992, having recently graduated, I was fortunate enough to participate in an encounter of over 1000 rural women in El Bierzo (Leon, Spain). This trip had a decisive impact on both my personal and intellectual life.

I discovered the strength and transformative possibilities of these women who did not have a university education, their capacity for organization in women's movements and their conviction that they could change the course of their lives. I learned that their reflections on the social transformation of gender relations were more profound than those I had had with other colleagues in the university. I was amazed by the procedures of their meetings and their tolerance for inclusion of everyone in the fight for common goals. I felt like an equal, talking and searching with them for shared victories.

I was invited on the trip by the women of the adult education center where I was collaborating and volunteering (Sánchez 1999). I had already begun experiencing the contrast between the feminist literature I had read and the problems of those "other women." Their protests were about more than just wage differences between businessmen and businesswomen. Their protests were about the inequalities and wage differences between businesspeople and "cleaning ladies."

When I returned home from El Bierzo, the women asked me not to forget their voices in my intellectual work. The women's movements that I had known and that I encountered subsequently in other places demonstrated to me that it is possible to work together to reorient the course of history toward an egalitarian perspective for the social transformation of gender relations; these women were already making it happen. I began to participate with enthusiasm and purpose in research in this field and in theoretical development and practical reflection through my involvement with some of these women's movements, with whom I continue to collaborate.

It was clear to me that it was necessary to set this analysis in the context of feminist theoretical work. It is through this social reality and from nonuniversity women and their movement that we are learning to develop, in academia, the dialogic feminist proposal that we present in this essay.

Feminism and the Achievements of Traditional Modernity

Prior to modernity, women were mere objects without a voice, incapable of being recognized as decision makers and always subject to the decisions that men (fathers, brothers, husbands) made for us. Along with the strong social hierarchies based on criteria of culture and economics (during the Middle Ages, attaining a dowry was one of the most frequent motives for financial assistance), women had to endure the added burden of gender discrimination. With women's obligation to be in the home, to care for their husband and children, an image of women as passive, obedient, and selfless was forged, which further impeded open access to public life, education, or any type of social, political, and economic participation. Social institutions not only silently observed this process, but in one way or another maintained it. For example, one can look at the relations between the church and courtly love. Monastic life was set along the guidelines that established an obvious parallel between love for a woman and faith in God. In monasteries, the image of woman, the object of attraction, was transformed into the Virgin Mary. In the chivalric ideal, the body of the woman was always considered unyielding; in some poems it is compared to a fortress, which alluded to Celestial Jerusalem (Leroux-Dhuys 1998). Also conserved are the vivid descriptions of the feelings of faith, which closely resembled sexual desire.

The Enlightenment radically changed this situation, which was now presented with the ideas, well known, that marked the widespread use of knowledge and a confidence in reason that modified relations with nature, history, and reality. The Enlightenment was fertile ground for the creation of a new conception of the person, who became increasingly more capable of transforming his/her environment and articulating his/her demands in social movements. Normally, this genesis of social agency is seen as the result of enlightened thought. However, we would like to indicate a reading of this historic episode in reverse. The networks of solidarity were the ones responsible for the appearance of this subjectification process. Modernity began to develop parallel to the attainment of its demands and public participation.

In modern times, ideas were born that were related to the need for freeing mankind from superstition and irrational religious impositions. Groups began to demand autonomy and the opportunity for social collectives to provide feasible proposals for change. Many ideas emerged that aimed at finding the natural equality of all people. However, the ability for action for men and women in traditional modernity was asymmetrical. Thus, many women's movements organized to fight for this equality, even at the risk of their lives. The freedom and equality that these women wanted was also extended by them to other groups.[1] Reason and truth, regardless of where they surfaced from, should have been independent of gender questions.

However, other types of hierarchies were generated in these social movements, the feminist movement included. Modernity became an all-encompassing project in which a small minority believed they held the truth. Consequently, when decision-making power was in the hands of a select few who were the "guides" of the ideas and the movement, the capacity of everyone else was held in doubt. Thus, trust in the reasoning capacity to perceive the truth was solely in the hands of a few leaders who oftentimes forgot, or simply confused, important issues that affected all women.

We pose an example of this. In Spain, women gained the right to vote in 1931. Clara Campoamor of the Radical Party, Victoria Kent of the Socialist Party, and Margarita Nelken of the Spanish Socialist Labor Party (PSOE) were the only women who participated in the parliamentary debate on the passage of female suffrage in the Second Republic. However, only Campoamor defended women's right to vote. Although the other two defended female suffrage on an ideological level, they did not support it politically, arguing that the vote could not be given to women who were ignorant and lacking in culture. Clara Campoamor declared that if the right to vote was to be denied women for a lack of culture, the same had to be done in the case of men without studies. Since this was not going to happen, women did achieve the right to vote, regardless of socioeconomic background (Capel 1975, Fagoaga 1985).

When today's women's movement forgets nonuniversity women's discourses, we can say that they are making the same mistake made by Kent and Nelken. A large part of past feminism considered that not all individuals were able to interpret their own reality and propose measures for transformation. We must stop this from happening again. It is incompatible with the idea of freedom and emancipation that these movements supposedly profess. The dynamics that limit the participation of all women in the movements they represent, by relegating responsibility to a theoretical and political elite, tend toward discipline as the only road to common actions. Additionally, responsibility of the people in the movement weakens, which, as the bureaucratic machine grows, becomes less efficient. This is when popular participation turns into election of representatives who decide for everyone.

It was during the nineteenth century that women began to view as feasible the possibility of creating a society based on equality. Education was seen as the first step toward achieving this goal,[2] and, since then, access to education has been one of the most important claims that women have made.[3] In traditional modernity, the academic woman appropriated the fight for all women, among them those who continue to be silent today. Thus, an elite generated interpretations of reality, defined strategies of action and decided who should participate and who was to be represented. The "feminism of equality" was born in this context, composed of feminist movements that emerged with a homogenizing vision in which only some women (the academics) were considered bearers of progressive values that had to be defended, while they defined forms of action that the rest of the women had to adopt.

In light of the achievements of the women's movement in the modern era, we recognize that despite the profound problems that were forgotten and the erroneous decisions that were made, the balance tips to the positive. In fact, a greater level of emancipation and independence accompanied the appearance of the New Woman. In the context of women's studies, this has occurred along with the gradual emergence of the idea of social agency, capable of transforming contexts through reflection (this aspect is discussed further in the next section).

A feminist movement such as "No means no," born out of issues of date rape in the United States, is an example of how it is possible to actively fight against the oppression of women and their sexual freedom on the basis of values of solidarity and equality, while bringing a societal menace to the fore for the whole population. This movement has provided a number of arguments to fight against situations in which some men continue to justify their sexual aggressions against women with the excuse that "she wanted it," "even if they say no, I know they like it," "she provoked me," etc. It has raised women's awareness, helped those of us who want to report gender-based violence and harassment, and pressured the justice system to confront this issue in a courageous way.

Feminist movements have made certain demands of their own, such as those of the women abolitionists who were rejected by the London antislavery convention. It is not by chance that International Women's Day (March 8) has its origins in and continues to commemmorate the women's labor movements of the late nineteenth and early twentieth centuries, which we all remember in the context of the devastating Triangle Shirtwaist Co. Fire in New York City in 1911, which killed 146 women textile workers. Although it is not clear exactly how the fire started, the owners of the company wanted to put an end to the women textile workers' protests and demands for better working conditions, an increase in salary, a reduction in work hours, and an end to exploitation, and were later charged with manslaughter. A victory for these women-led labor movements at hide tide and on the front lines of the industrial age would have been a tremendous achievement for mass society.

Time has shown us how, due to these initiatives, women have been able to access different political, social, and economic spheres, and we can say that relations between the genders are better today than they were in the past, which has been the legacy of pioneering feminism. With the advent of modernity, woman became an agent, and thereby acquired the capacity for action and transformation.[4] Solidarity united with agency led us to organize ourselves in order to achieve all that had been taken from us. Thanks to the values of modernity (equality, freedom, and solidarity), the feminist movements demonstrated women's capacity to organize and claim our obvious rights, such as the right to vote, remuneration for domestic work, access to education, and the elimination of the "droit du seigneur" (the lord's right). It was social movements, among them feminism, that were the real catalysts of the Enlightenment, demanding and bringing into practice the values of modernity.

Feminism in the Face of the Crisis of Modernity

From here on we will trace the crisis of modernity and attempts to overcome it. The importance of this point is essential, since the different ways of overcoming modernity have had important implications in the course of feminist movements.

We have highlighted the process of modernization and illustrated the main lines that articulated its social agenda and its possibility for change. Accordingly, we have seen that in modernity important achievements were attained in women's lives. However, traditional modernity has also demonstrated a less friendly face. The modern institutions have been directed toward and by a privileged group of people, generating exclusion and injustices based on age, ethnicity, and gender (see Alcoba 2001 on art and museums). The masculinity of the system has been hegemonic in traditional modernity, as reflected in culture, politics, and in many other public spheres.

The confirmation of this reality provoked a very radical position against modernity in which the reasons for the failure of the Enlightenment were not analyzed. The movements that surfaced in reaction demolished anything that had any affiliation to modernity, its values, its principles, its foundation in reason. All that energy expended against modernity resulted in no alternatives being proposed, since the transforming subject that traditional modernity presented us with had been destroyed along with it.

The paradox is that we understand this crisis of conscience as the result of modernity's reflections on itself, as a function of an unprecedented desire for self-awareness and of self-assurance. It was this self-reflection, culminating in the last quarter of the twentieth century, that provoked the urgency to overcome modernity.[5] Thus, we find modernity submitted to the following astonishing dynamic: It has developed as it has dissolved, which means that attempts to move beyond it have come from its own self-awareness, which simultaneously generates estrangement. For instance, the questioning of the aspects of traditional modernity's "less friendly face," as mentioned above—gender roles and vestiges of the hierarchy that predated the modern era, which had to be transformed—was itself typically modern. It is in this vein that we can interpret the sexual ambiguity with which many literary authors and painters at the end of the nineteenth and the beginning of the twentieth century, such as Lesbia Brandon (de Diego 1992), debated. Currently, there are different processes of overcoming traditional modernity and its philosophy centered on a subject as creator of meaning, which has revealed itself to be completely imperfect. On the one hand, postmodern positions acknowledge the failure of the principles and institutions of the Enlightenment, welcoming the death of the subject, dissolving the reference points established by reason, discrediting the role of human agency, and thus limiting the power of social change, which becomes constrained by the abstract will of the system (rather than the actions of individuals who compose it). Meanwhile, some authors defend the possibilities of modernity that remain unexplored and welcome a "second modernity," in which the processes that are unfinished and have brought many benefits for humanity are radicalized. These social achievements took place due to the modern appearance of a social subject capable of changing the course of history (Flecha, Gómez, and Puigvert 2001).

The thought of the Enlightenment, reflexive by nature, endows people with a capacity for action as social subjects. When reason is applied to the past, tradition, and history, we begin to suspect that we do not necessarily need to be their victims, that we can modify our relationship to them, and that social transformation is possible. We must interpret the first women's suffrage movements of the nineteenth century in this sense. Therefore, even as we attribute importance to the need to redefine a thought centered on the subject, we believe that postmodern attempts to annul human agency have undesirable consequences for people. We cite the negative effects that the rise of postmodernism had in the 1980s, diminishing initiatives of women's groups and contributing to confrontations among them.[6] Behind the apparent sexual transparency of postmodernism, we note, for example, the absence of female artists in the first exhibitions of postmodern art in London ("A New Spirit in Painting," the Royal Academy, 1981) and New York, where in 1984 there were feminist demonstrations in front of the MoMA denouncing this omission.[7] Contemplating the social subject also entails contemplating the possibility of transforming reality. By upholding the disappearance of the subject, postmodernism plays into a paradigm that is not only futile with respect to social transformation, but also reactionary with respect to women.

Efforts to overcome a philosophy centered on the subject and the questioning of the traditional referents on which modernity was based have been grounded in the guidelines of the "linguistic turn," which gives preeminence to the *meaning* of the reference over the perspectives of the bases. Therefore, in its proclamation of the death of the subject and criticism of any attempt to establish universalistic and rational categories, the linguistic turn has emphasized that which is relative in thought, the absence of stable references, and therefore the impossibility of agreement and dialogue. To the contrary, we defend the principle of a "second modernity" or a "dialogic modernity," and we insist on the capacity of reason and reflection to construct what is social, articulating a program defined by the mechanisms of language and speech, but far from the sense in which these are meant by relativism. Instead, dialogue becomes the key element for a sustainable society in which differences are possible. For us, any suspicion of "essentialism" (Rorty 1989) is nullified by the principle of dialogue that rewrites the complex relations between theory and reality and defines concepts in a consensual, temporal, and gradual manner. In the following section, we will go deeply into the ample subject that we at the Center for Social and Educational Research (CREA) in Barcelona define as the "dialogic turn."

The crisis of subjectivity, inspired by the Nietzschean program and artistic modernism, led to structuralist and poststructuralist movements by way of the formulations of Lévi-Strauss, the linguistic turn, and Foucault. Certain implications of the primacy of language will contribute to the dissolution of the modern subject. If the annihilation in modern Foucauldian thought were to reach its zenith, we would conclude, as Foucault writes, that "man would erase himself." We cannot forget that the death of the subject, of its entity and identity, implies the impossibility of knowledge, dialogue, and action. In light of this, on what bases can women articulate their social demands? How can we gain spaces that up until now have been denied us? On the other hand, the Foucauldian alliance between knowledge and aspirations of power eliminates arguments of the legitimacy of many of the demands made by women, which can be viewed as "more of the same": merely an attempt at gaining a position of power that up until now has been for others. The disappearance of the notion of subjectivity is also central to Derrida, the most enthusiastic defender of the linguistic turn. In his criticism of phonocentrism and his defense of the written word, this author in effect destroys the possibility of expression and authorship. With the disappearance of intent and the end of reflexive conscience, social achievements become mere accidents, and progress an illusion. How does one interpret change without a *dual* interpretation of society, in which all women can influence the structures? For Bourdieu (2000), women have assumed, or internalized, a masculine domination, as transmitted through the social institutions of the Enlightenment (church, state, school), through language, and through a symbolic violence. From the standpoint of this deep submission, any resistance to masculine domination would be understood as the failure of the feminine or, even more, the nonexistence of the specifically feminine (while there are authors who, like Bourdieu, are capable of seeing something that we do not see). How can women escape from this cycle if what is masculine pervades everything? How can we control our own destiny if, once structuralism dismisses the subject, social change is a reflection only of the *structural* possibilities of our society? We conclude that structuralism paralyzes social transformations.

Foucault's thought opens itself to irrationality. Beginning with the end of modernity and subjectivity, language precedes any construction of the subject, since it orders our experience and builds our illusion of subjectivity. This idea of language, the arbitrariness of the Nietzschean-inspired moral order, the disdain for modern references, and siding with irrational experiences (dreams, madness) were used by Foucault as excuses to transgress and be as nonconformist as possible. Liberating thought from the prison of reason is simply very impractical for Afghani women who are trying to eliminate social barriers that oppress them. This poetic and undefined openness to irrationality being connected to the idea of transgression, Foucault is influenced by Sade and Bataille. How many women would aim to be objects of desire of the former and victims of heterogeneous impulse of the latter?

Every time that postmodern, deconstructionist, and genealogical thought have occupied a place in academia (to which it seemed to be opposed), in a sort of new exclusionary rationality, feminism has suffered, especially in its capacity to articulate viable proposals for social change. Some of the victories obtained in the past have been made relative by interpreting them as a turn toward the possession of power rather than as a fundamental debt restored to women's dignity as human beings. From this perspective, more egalitarian access to education or to the labor market can be viewed as a submission to the masculine vision of the world, with the objective of gaining power. Largely believing in the demolition of validity claims would imply a great weakening in the arguments through which the feminist movement has articulated its voice, which would always be under suspicion of obeying power strategies. The relativization of feminist objectives has even arrived at considering women's power as being precisely at the point that previously was a symptom of their own oppression. In this most sordid viewpoint, truth and lie, justice and injustice are matters of points of view, breaking from the tendency of feminism in modernity to demand that women's rights be extended to all people, independent of culture, sexual orientation, age, etc. (Irigaray 1994, Nicholson 1997). To this relativist feminist viewpoint, where dialogue is understood as the confrontation of aspirations of power, equality is not only impossible, but also undesirable.

This is from where the "feminism of difference" emerges, focused on revealing the characteristics that separate the genders (on a physical, biological, cognitive level) and the impossibility of equality. This led to the negation of values and victories for which feminists had fought; to defend equality, solidarity, or the feelings of the subject was considered moralistic, repressive, antiliberating, and, consequently, antifeminist. Many of the followers of the feminism of difference collaborated in this, breaking the ties of solidarity that many other women had struggled for. They presented the rejection of the values of the Enlightenment as the alternative that would provide women a way out of patriarchal society.

Some linguistic studies biased regarding gender issues are full of generalizations and symbolic evidences that even in the most convincing cases are no more than just "assumptions." Some of these authors could very well believe that inequalities are inevitable and therefore the solution is not to put an end to them at all, but to invert the order with respect to men, to use an *other* conceptual hierarchy, opposed to the masculine (prostitution, castration). This may lead us to ask ourselves: What is the use of these ideas for overcoming the real oppression of millions of women? Their vagueness, unattainable nature, assimilation of inequality, defense of the impossibility of dialogue or social transformation (a denial based on the end of the social subject), etc., could lead only to indifference and anomie.

There has definitely been confusion between conceptions of liberation and proposals for transgression, which in practice have paralyzed the feminist movement's capacity for action and accentuated the hermeticism of feminist discourse for the majority of women. Confused with the expression of absolute freedom, transgression has been an ideal to which the left as well as the feminist movement have been strongly allied during many different historical moments. A rupture with the public order leaves the space open to the will of the one who transgresses and takes himself/herself as the sole purpose. In practice, the result has been considerably negative. Normally, totalitarian periods of the modern era (Italian fascism, the Nazi regime, etc.) have been preceded by such transgressive ideas (e.g., futurism), which are apparently defenders of freedom. With regard to women, we believe that it is a fallacy to defend pornography as a transgression of common moral values without considering it another manifestation of the reification of women that tends to reflect violent and humiliating behaviors to which we are still submitted.

Ignored Contributions:
Women's Movements in Solidarity

Today's societies are more and more dialogic (Flecha, Gómez, and Puigvert 2001). Information societies are the symbolic context in which dialogue is penetrating social, political, personal, and other relations. If formerly the king was inheritor of power by virtue of God, today it is the government by virtue of the votes of the citizenry. The same has occurred with personal relationships: If formerly we had to accept arranged marriages, nowadays an increasing number of couples talk about and negotiate the kind of relationship they want and the tasks that each person will take on.

Obviously, this dialogic movement has limitations imposed on it by dominant groups that build barriers and complicate dialogic transformations. There are women obligated to not vote or to vote by obligation, there are women who bear abuse and unjust treatment from their partners without any opportunity for dialogue. But this does not mean that we are moving toward less dialogic societies, but that the road is long and difficult and we must continue struggling so that dialogue is increasingly the prevailing practice. Dialogic modernity does not limit our alternatives; it offers more possibilities. It does not mean choosing between marriage or being alone, but raises all the possibilities decided upon by everyone who participates in dialogue on an egalitarian basis.

As we described earlier, the growth of feminist movements contributed to the development of numerous practices that transformed many women's lives and others' images of them as they became active agents in the course of history. However, although in this process we fought for achieving higher rates of women's participation in all spheres, these universal principles were articulated in very particular ways that forgot the needs of broad sectors of the very diverse women among them. These principles were imposed as the sole and universal truth, without including diversity. From this conception, as mentioned earlier, homogenizing practices were promoted that underestimated the social, cultural, and individual differences of women. Emancipation, the initial aim of the feminist struggle, was diverted from its ultimate goal, given that it gave way to imposing a model that aimed "to open the eyes" of the rest of women. If we listen to these women, however, we would hear them declaring:

Women with university degrees are not the only ones who hold the truth. . . . All truths must be listened to. . . . University graduates should not create a glass box and should come down and see that com mon women—those who are not university graduates—have the same problems, and at times they are very difficult problems, very big ones that university-graduate women need to know about as well. (From a nonacademic women's group)

Given the need for addressing the differences that had been ignored, a trend within feminism was born that was no longer concerned with equality. From that moment on, existing inequalities between women were "respected," and an egalitarian recognition of differences was not promoted. The arrival of postmodernism in social movements, explained in the second section, broke many ties of solidarity and confirmed an error: to believe that abandoning the positive values that were won by women was the only way to defend against the homogenization that traditional modernity presented.

However, nowadays many women's movements are demanding to be able to enjoy the victories achieved by their predecessors while simultaneously ensuring respect for and fostering of their differences. This is the case in the fight to end the suppression of voices of dissent in the name of the purity of a culture based in religion. In Afghanistan, the Taliban drove the whole civil population into a state of terrified silence that has since their downfall been denounced. During their reign, many women participated in RAWA (the Revolutionary Association of the Women of Afghanistan), which fought so that access to education and health care could be extended to all women and did not have to be carried out precariously in clandestine ways. Thus, they shared their struggle with many women's movements from other countries while also reaffirming their aim and determination to be respected as followers of Islam.

In March 2001, when the political debate about the two millennial Buddhist statues in Afghanistan was raised, RAWA wanted to make women's situation visible. The decapitation and destruction of these statues, which belonged to the universal artistic patrimony, awoke greater international outrage than did the defense of social rights that are also the patrimony of all humanity. The artistic debate eclipsed and diverted attention from the rest of the savageries committed upon a completely silenced and forgotten population, among whom the women were the most neglected. During the meeting in Islamabad between UN secretary-general Kofi Annan and the Afghani foreign minister to avoid the destruction of the statues, a large number of women were at the doors of the meeting with the clear intention of also including the Afghani women's situation into the debate and denouncing the systematic violation of human rights in Afghanistan. Taking a postmodern position, feminists would have defended nonintervention in Afghanistan as well as nonextension of the basic principles that guarantee respect, dignity, and the channels of expression for its women.

The "other women" are all those who have been left out of our discourses and feminist struggles because they are not academics or they belong to cultural minorities, that is to say, the immense majority of women are excluded from the formulation of priorities and themes selected by the movement that academics and Western women have created (Puigvert 2001). These "other women" reject at the grassroots level both those who decide what all women must do and those who criticize them for not doing what is imposed on them by a supposed liberation. They are making contributions that they insist must be included in our debates:

> Women who fight to defend their rights from privileged situations have to affirm their solidarity for all women and situations of injustice. (Federation of Cultural and Adult Education Associations [FACEPA] women's group)

This is possible in the spaces of solidarity they create, in which they look for understanding based on the plurality of the existing voices, contrasting the differences and reflecting on how to lessen the inequalities that all women face. In this way, the options for liberation are not imposed by some women on others, but are defined and created communally through horizontal communication among everyone:

> Maybe they [the feminists], since they believe that they have already overcome certain things, do not realize the other needs that we have. . . . The way to realize them is by talking, opening up dialogue— if not, then nothing. Then we can get what we lack, because maybe they think they have achieved some issues that they really have not. (A nonacademic woman)

From relationships based on respect and understanding of our diverse identities and experiences, many women who had historically been under submission to masculine forms of domination began to question their assumptions, to exchange meanings between each other, and analyze alternative messages and styles. Together they reflected on the nature of their role, questioned their experiences, and planned strategies for change. They turned from being women without any alternatives or mere observers of change into active protagonists of social transformation with regard to gender relations.

> There are women who go to meetings and we get there thinking that we are not male chauvinist, but when we learn from the others, we realize that it is true, that my opinion is wrong, I am damaging myself with my ideas, and from others' ideas you discover that you are doing things that are damaging to yourself, you discover things that you hadn't realized that . . . this is happening to you and the other one is telling you that she is fed up with it . . . and you were assuming them as your own, as normal things, and when listening to her, by her complaining . . . well I think that is what I am doing, then I have to do and say something . . . to her. . . . (A nonacademic woman)

The common principles yet different realities of the "other women" bring up a contradiction in the very values of modernity. These women realize that access to public space traditionally monopolized by men is not enough to guide the transformation in gender relations. That is why they generate more egalitarian dynamics of communication and spaces for dialogue, in order to reach consensus about how they want to live so that the plurality of their voices is respected.

For example, the women participating in the Zapatista movement in Chiapas state in Mexico are at the same time critical of their inequalities. The Zapatista movement regained strength following the uprising on January 1, 1994, demanding the dignity and right to participate in Mexican society on an equal basis and on the basis of the indigenous particularity of the Maya people. In this context, indigenous women have also organized themselves in order to participate on an equal basis *within* the Zapatista movement.

In 1994, women of the Tzotziles, Tzeltales, Tojolabales, and Mames indigenous (Maya) groups met in San Cristóbal de las

Casas (Chiapas) in the workshop Rights of Women in Our Customs and Traditions. They demanded respect as indigenous people but also as women, and not only from the Mexican government, but from their partners in the guerrilla movement as well. Since childhood, they had been taught to obey and not to protest. They now decided not to keep quiet any longer and to demand equal participation in the elaboration of laws and in how to reformulate the articles of the Mexican Constitution, so that indigenous people, both men and women, would have a stake in the laws. In this meeting they also demanded participation in decision making by having positions in the community and in the existing organizations, as well as an increase in the number of schooled girls. All these claims were guided by the will to actively participate in the social transformation that the Zapatista struggle signified for the indigenous population.

Due largely to the struggle of grassroots women's groups, institutions within the labor, educational, and professional systems are forced to take new approaches in order to adapt themselves to a more flexible and dialogic society, where communication and dialogue are key elements for addressing current social changes and influencing the radicalization of democracy.

> As we have said at other times, education is essential and we have to educate our children so that it is possible to imagine things differently than they have traditionally been. (FACEPA women's group)

These "other women" who have established more egalitarian dynamics for interaction state that they never set out for a feminist fight—they found themselves immersed in it. Although they did not have an example or rules to follow as a model, they did know clearly that they did not want to be relegated to second place as they had been until then. Their lives had changed, and not particularly because feminist theoreticians had opened alternatives to the lives they had been faced with earlier.

> I thought I wasn't feminist. When I heard the radical feminists . . . and it turns out that, after thinking and thinking, I believe I have been a feminist since I was born. . . . Since I was young, there were things I didn't like . . . but I didn't know that this was feminist. Since I have been with this movement for transformation, I thought that I've always been a feminist. (A nonacademic woman)

There exist groups of nonacademic and academic women who have initiated jointly the creation of spaces of solidarity grown out of informal meetings among friends or classmates, who want to feel more supported and wish to share their concerns and ideas with other women like themselves in order to begin—from this complicity—the social transformation of gender relations. These experiences prove that "other women" are generating knowledge. A new feminist discourse comes from the dialogic turn and has led these women to create different spaces of solidarity that can guide academics as to where the feminism of the twenty-first century should be heading. Some other examples of these movements and women's groups are the following:

The Research Network: Popular Women and Education

The Research Network was born in 1999 with the aim of establishing an active cooperation among researchers who work in specific fields of adult education at their respective universities. Although composed of academic women, this group works with and for women with low academic levels, who do not have university degrees. It seeks to promote knowledge about new formulas for social participation for nonacademic women, recognizing—through research—their cultural diversity. It focuses on the development of radical theories that allow for the creation of channels of social participation and the radicalization of democracy through the extension of lifelong education and training for women with low academic levels or without any formal education.

FACEPA Women's Group

FACEPA is a federation of adult-education associations in Catalonia that manage their own projects. It seemed unfair to them that educators and politicians decided about their education and their future without even asking them for their opinion. They wanted to break away from the elitist idea that they "do not know" about these things. The women's group emerged from the federation to specifically address women's issues. It meets once a month, sharing experiences, information, and knowledge about preselected issues: They want to break away from a low self-image, gain a voice, and prevent the appropriation of their feminism by women who would explain to them how they should act. Their meetings are based on spaces of egalitarian dialogue among women of different generations, cultures, and academic levels, grounded in their interests, knowledge, and experiences.

Drom Kotar Mestipen (Women's Gypsy Association)

This association was founded in 1999 as a result of the dialogue between Gypsy and non-Gypsy women of diverse ages and characteristics with the common goal of working for equality and against the discrimination of the Roma people. It is grounded in the principles of the equality of differences and egalitarian dialogue among all women. Since its inception, the association has participated in diverse forums in order to make known its objectives, in addition to participating in research projects about the Gypsy woman.[8] These objectives include: to work for equality and nondiscrimination between men and women within the Roma community; to overcome the racism and sexism that cause the dual inequality suffered by Gypsy women; to collaborate with all of the groups that fight for an equality that includes the right to maintain and develop differences; and to enhance the Gypsy woman's image as a transmitter and proponent of Roma cultural identity.

Mothers of the Plaza de Mayo (Argentina)

This group of mothers of *desaparecidos* started acting after the disappearances of young Argentines in 1974 and 1975 and the establishment of the dictatorship in Argentina in 1976. They protested against the Ministry of the Interior, the police, the church, and political parties. They are a model for the struggle and resistance of women who have never given up demanding justice.

Since those meetings begun in the Plaza de Mayo in Buenos Aires, at which the women organized themselves to go to the police and the interior ministry and to look for more mothers who had sons and daughters who had disappeared, they have had many public actions demanding a stop to negligence and that matters be addressed until all occurrences are verified and that justice is done. Women united as mothers and, having suffered the cruelty of a dictatorship, organized and became strong; that is why this movement is a reference worldwide. Currently, they direct the Popular University of the Mothers of the Plaza de Mayo, which offers studies on human rights, protest struggles, journalism, etc.

MEI al-Hanan (Women for Intercultural Education)

The Mujeres por una Educacion Intercultural is a group that springs from the desire of Islamic women to collaborate in the creation of new forms of communication between people and cultural groups that live in Barcelona and Catalonia. (*Al-Hanan* means "tenderness" or "affection.") Through their work, a group of women from different origins have decided to stimulate a truly intercultural dialogue, boosting cooperative learning and mutual recognition. They are grounded in an open, respectful, and positive attitude toward diversity, advocating exchange and knowledge through the daily networks that people weave in the spirit of solidarity.

Insha Allah

This is an association of Muslim women from different countries and with diverse academic levels. They fight for the recognition of their culture and advocate an interpretation of Islam that is oriented toward gender equality. Working toward this claim, in October 2000 in Barcelona they organized the first Conference of Muslim Women. Participating were women from diverse origins—from Africa, Europe, America, and Asia—who had settled in various parts of Spain and had assumed Islam at some point in their lives. The issues that they dealt with in terms of equality were: noncompetitive relations between the genders, the possibility for an enhanced participation of women in the economy, the fight against stereotypes and abuse by the mass media, family planning, education of children, and training in computer literacy and communication on the Internet.

We are witnessing how women from many different origins

and backgrounds are moving forward together toward social transformation in gender relations. As part of their struggle, associations such as the ones mentioned here are demanding access to the channels of participation in order to define and reach a consensus on human rights in terms of upholding the principle of equality based on the recognition of diversity (de Botton 2000).

These movements, and ultimately all the horizontal relations among women oriented toward mutual learning and respect, break away from the barriers that the "other women" feel. Academic reason does not prevail by discrediting discourses based on experience or women's direct knowledge; rather, academia and experiential knowledge complement each other. The Declaration of Rights of Participants in Adult Education, elaborated by FACEPA through a discursive process, proposes the right of all people without academic training to participate in educational processes, in order to avoid being supplanted by professionals and those who have already had this training.[9] At the same time, these groups allow for the extension of communication spaces to new places. These spaces usually improve in direct relation to the level of involvement by the women, given that they become active participants where they used to attend only to be lectured to.

The joint action of all women is aimed at the attainment of spaces and processes of dialogue and mutual learning in which all the voices are included. In the last part of this paper, we make the case for dialogic feminism and discuss the concept of the *equality of differences* as key to the inclusion of the plurality of voices.

⚇

Equality cannot be mistaken for homogenization, but it must guarantee the respect of each one of us to live according to our choices. Traditional modernity proclaimed the objective of equality, but based its concept in only Western culture, without entering into dialogue with others. In order to radicalize democracy, it is necessary to overcome the imposition of a "universal" that has not been discussed by everybody. The movements of the "other women" are based on the victories of modernity as the foundation for a new society, proposing that in the new century we must rewrite modernity. They do this by returning to the very values of solidarity and equality that were already present in it.

In their reflections and practices, they question policies that result in the preservation of majority-culture hegemony, and insist that these policies, in order to allow free choice, provide the same ability for people from minority cultural groups to enrich or even deny the characteristics of their own culture. Women's emancipation is unthinkable without cultural transmission, in the same way that we cannot obviate the cultural protest that contributes to the transformation of cultures. This fact questions the so-called authenticity of cultures, since they are not static, and even less so in the current process of globalization. Current societies are already racially mixed. The challenge of the multicultural society therefore consists not only in respect for and recognition of cultural diversity, but also in generating more egalitarian gender relations in experiences of diversity. Arabic, Muslim, Latin American, African, Asian, and Native American women, along with progressive antiracist movements in general, particularly ground their struggle in the equality of differences.

In November 2000, the 4th Gypsy Community: From Equality We Conquer Rights conference was held in Madrid. It was highlighted there that participation is the strategy to use for the promotion of the Gypsy woman, so that, through her cultural affirmation, a more egalitarian society for everyone can be reached. Roma women from different origins and academic levels attended the conference and demonstrated their mobilization, proclaiming equality through identity. No longer would they be forced to choose between becoming *paya* (the feminine form *[paya/payo]* of the word Gypsies use to refer to non-Gypsy people) or suffering exclusion and discrimination due to their retained identity. This homogenizing equality does not solve the social problems of all of the women belonging to cultural minorities; instead, it builds many obstacles to their inclusion, leading in this way to a double discrimination (of gender and culture).

Even though women from minority or non-Western backgrounds are fighting for the same rights of equality (in education, the labor market, and other public spaces) as are women's groups of the majority European and North American cultures, they are doing it to build a modernity that has been reinterpreted and reshaped with their own cultural references.

All this expresses the huge diversity of approaches existing within these societies. In this sense, the veil, the *hijab*, cannot be regarded exclusively as the symbol of confinement; it can also be the symbol of liberation. This plurality is illustrated by the different meanings that Muslim women give to it:

> In the same way that many women attended the demonstrations veiled in order to defend their Muslim identity, many others [. . .] removed their veil with the same intention: Islam was so egalitarian that it allowed them to give up the *hijab*. (Aixalá, 2000: 266)

This example was clearly witnessed in Istanbul, when university women who attended classes wearing the *hijab* were required to discard this traditional form of dress—which, according to the university officials, was a symbol of the oppression of women characteristic of "fundamentalist Islam"—if they wanted to continue their education. It aroused the indignation of many and very diverse women in Istanbul, generating enormous solidarity. Their answer was not long in coming: The street was witness to the protest demonstrations that Aixalá alludes to, which saw a gathering of great diversity of ideological and religious positions and lifestyles demanding freedom.

The Feminist Theory of the Twenty-First Century: Toward Dialogic Feminism[10]

The challenge that we have set out for feminism is to take up and theorize the dynamics and proposals that are being formulated by the popular women's and minority women's movements like the ones discussed above. These movements are bringing out a number of gaps and inconsistencies that we feminist academics have in our discourse, and these criticisms force us to progress in the orientation of the theoretical debate. From egalitarian dialogue and exchange between the "other women" and academic women, together, we can reorient democracy toward a feminism that encompasses the full diversity of our experiences and interests. This is possible if, with egalitarian dialogue, we are able to break through the restricted areas of feminism that we have constructed. Some sectors of "other women" have been demanding this type of dialogue for a long time.

Women, through our claims, have been gaining spaces and identities that were once taken away from us because of gender. We are now raising a voice that in the twenty-first century almost nobody dares to question. However, a minority of women with university degrees and high-skilled jobs have progressively hegemonized our movements. The struggles and worries in the daily lives of "other women" have often little to do with the reality that academic women end up describing.

The struggles and voices of "other women" delegitimize the perspectives that consider women as lacking the judgment to articulate the issues and oppose the elements that limit their freedom, from which only a few, already emancipated women can save them. Despite all the obstacles that we (academics) have placed to prevent these women from being heard, they have demonstrated in their daily lives the capacity to fight and transform. And what is even more important is that they are having a decisive impact on what will be, without a doubt, the future of a radically transformational feminism. As we have seen throughout this essay, there are many women's groups and groups from different cultures that are creating spaces in which they propose to be more united not only among each other but also with all women. This egalitarian dialogue decisively strengthens all of the changes that are taking place in their contexts.

The egalitarian transformation of their daily lives should be taken in and assumed by feminism and academic women, since they are proposing to radicalize the concept of equality, to overcome homogenizing interpretations, and include the plurality of voices (to incorporate the aspirations of women of different academic and cultural levels).

The dialogue and respect that each of us is capable of came not through a college or university degree, or through studies, but through what we learned throughout life, experience. . . . In our group nobody has a university degree. (A nonacademic woman)

The inclusion of all voices in egalitarian dialogue among all women in the feminist debate will allow us to move toward the theoretical development of what we believe should be the feminism of the twenty-first century: dialogic feminism, which aims to unite the efforts of all women (of different educational levels, ethnicities, and social classes) to overcome the inequalities we face.

This is framed, as mentioned above, in the dialogic turn that has taken place in today's society. Dialogic modernity is what enables us to orient our joint actions toward the equality of differences. It allows different women to be able to live together in the same territories and with equal rights that do not endanger, but reinforce and enrich their respective identities.

In order for dialogic feminism to succeed, there must be (1) the radicalization of the principles of modernity and (2) trust in the efforts of all women to change history.

The Radicalization of the Principles of Modernity

We understand that feminism and postmodernism are not intellectually or politically allied. Instead, the former reinforces people's possibilities in our democratic and feminist victories, while the latter undermines these possibilities and displaces our transformational aspirations, both theoretically and practically. The feminism that was captivated by postmodernism led to situations that remind us of certain inequalities we had already overcome:

> There are sometimes those who do the same, they abuse other people that, that they feel bad for. I remember when I began to work in another place. I had a very bad cold. . . . I could not go to work. . . . I called first thing in the morning and uy!, she said all sorts of stuff . . . and when I went there, she didn't talk to me . . . there was a change . . . very bad treatment. . . . She even reminded me of the meal . . . and I told her: I'm sorry but I'm not a slave . . . she became pale with fury. . . . I felt very bad. . . . It hurt me very much, she seemed like a very educated, professional girl. (A nonacademic woman)

The central statement that we propose in dialogic feminism is the defense of radicalizing democratic processes in order to elaborate a theory together that allows for only one definition of femininity. One that is understood not as homogeneous but inclusive, dynamic, and egalitarian for all the voices. That is to say, a femininity that takes gender differences into account, rather than fostering their disappearance, that is sensitive to the context, rather than indifferent to the situations.

> *There is a distance between the objectives of our progressive movements and the daily realities of women. Yet, through the links of*

solidarity and egalitarian dialogue, we are making efforts to accomplish the principles agreed upon, which are progressively transforming realities.

At the same time that the feminism of difference, in a mistaken attempt to not succumb to an essentialist discourse about gender, attacks the approaches that attempt to reach agreement through a dialogue that is increasingly more egalitarian, it also defends a multiplicity of opinions, not for the purpose of reaching agreement but simply so they can exist alongside each other, without any communication or coordinated joint actions to transform gender relations and society in general. This approach, which we reject, leads to the deactivation of movements and of women as transforming agents. The one we propose presents the power of dialogue, through egalitarian procedures based on reflection and argumentation—both theoretical as well as from life—rather than on the position of the people who defend it.

> When a woman gains power she might change, why do we want her in power? We want her in power to defend us [. . .] When a woman gains power she should never forget that she is a woman [. . .] Sometimes women who reach high positions forget to continue fighting for the rights of those who are still in situations of inequality. (FACEPA women's group)

Trust in the Action of All Women to Change the Course of History

In terms of feminist theory it has been considered unnecessary up until now to open the dialogue to the plurality of voices that we represent. Feminist discourse is considered to be the exclusive birthright of university women. As we have seen, the social sciences with a dialogic orientation question the role of the expert. This debate has not yet had enough influence on feminist theories. However, the dialogic movements of the "other women" are clear about it: They want to actively participate in the decision-making process.

Many of these nonuniversity women (socialized according to the standards of behavior they have historically assumed) were used to "fulfilling their duties" at home, taking care of the family, without any kind of autonomy, much less any possibility for action. In the spaces that we mentioned earlier, these women begin to question their way of thinking and come to modify them from the interpretations and points of view of other women. In this way, they demand from academic feminists their right to participate in the elaboration of feminist theory. Many women who have historically been subjected to masculine domination go from being women without any alternatives, or at best, objects of change, to being the protagonists of their own social transformation with respect to gender relations.

> Life is getting modern and you cannot stay behind. (A nonacademic woman)

The hegemonic approach that has consistently silenced the voices of nonacademic women is being replaced by a dialogic perspective oriented toward creating spaces and learning processes and dialogue (Flecha 2000) in which all voices are included, with the objective of facilitating interrelationship, respect, and the transformation of gender relations. From this perspective, women go from being passive consumers to cultural producers and agents of transformation.

⚋

Many women (both nonacademic and academic) are already promoting the dialogic orientation of education.[11] They are doing this along with the social theories of this very perspective—in the international debate of the feminist movement, the dialogic dynamics of the "other women" are translated into theories of solidarity.

From dialogic feminism and through the joint action of all women, we believe that it is possible to overcome two of the limitations assumed by current feminist perspectives. Dialogic feminism leaves behind the traditional debate about equality vs. difference, taking the assumption instead that the only way to defend equality is by means of respect and listening to the diverse voices. On these terms, the theoretical development of the concept of the equality of differences articulates spaces of dialogue and egalitarian exchange.

In opposition to the feminists who mistook equality for homogenization, aiming to extend the reality of the academic

Western woman to all women, other feminists emerged who rejected the model that defends difference. In this way, enormous inequalities were justified and the feminist movement was paralyzed, breaking ties of solidarity and egalitarian exchange among women.

However, as demonstrated by many women's movements, equality and difference are not contradictory concepts. The defense of equality would be unthinkable if the plurality of voices were not incorporated. All women have the same right to live differently. It is from this perspective of solidarity that we focus the debate, in coordinated struggles upon which we are together in agreement, in order to overcome the barriers that the social structures have been trying to impose upon us for centuries.

The explosion of the feminist movement in traditional modernity helped to overcome many inequalities in gender relations. But there are still many inequalities to be questioned, rejected, and transformed, which can be challenged today in a public debate due to the dialogic turn taking place in society. The concept of the equality of differences allows us to elaborate a proposal that provides us all with the freedom to choose how and what we want to be, while promoting ties of solidarity between all people and us.

The urgent need for feminism to incorporate the plurality of women's voices is not due solely to the growth of multicultural societies but to the fact that these societies increasingly require the voice of every woman and not just that of an academic minority. It is necessary to include in the feminist debate the presence of collectives and people from other cultures (Gypsies, Arabs, Latinas . . .) and to do it from their own social, economic, and educational positions. Today, active participation of the citizenry is not just possible but desirable as an element that reinforces and radicalizes democracy. The "other women" are already doing it, and it is precisely their plurality of voices that is continuously contributing to reshape their movements.

Overcoming these two limits gives the women's movement a key dimension in the transformation of gender relations in all spheres of social life. Feminist discourse usually monopolized by the university elite is beginning to feel the pressure of the "other women's" voices, directly through their own organizations as well as indirectly by means of the dialogic theories that are beginning to have a growing influence in our theoretical debates. In the feminist conference held in Córdoba in December 2000 called Feminismo. Es . . . y será [Feminism Is . . . and Will Be], we could already appreciate how these demands were becoming a reality. The conference was opened with a video, whose title even had an impact on us: *Invisible Women.* The video showed the stories of different women, married, widowed, with children, Gypsy . . . all of them nonacademic women, with daily struggles to survive in a world that has excluded them and made them invisible. Two of the women who appeared in the video entered the room, and the emotion and applause that was heard in the hall was already evidence that feminism was changing.

Dialogic feminism proposes to academics, a minority of women, to stop feeling like they are the exclusive owners of feminist knowledge and to share this space with the critical contributions that the "other women" are already developing. This will imply an enriching process: to conduct research in close contact with women who, until recently, we have seen as inferior or whom we simply ignored. This process proposes that we be committed intellectuals involved in grassroots movements and close to the concerns and contributions of the "other women."

Dialogic feminism is a proposal that aims to generate important ties of solidarity that allow for the transformation of gender relations and the development of theoretical elements that help us to foster a feminism that has a leading role in the twenty-first century.

Notes

1. Many women's movements defended equality not only between women and men, but also for other groups. For example, the abolitionist women who were rejected by the men at the World Anti-Slavery Convention in London in 1840 sparked the well-known Seneca Falls (New York) Women's Rights Convention (1848). At that convention, social equality for both women and slaves was demanded.

2. A good example of this is the anarchist feminist movement Free Women (Mujeres Libres), which emerged in Madrid and Barcelona in 1936. These women emphasized access to culture as the way to overcome social barriers that face women. The education and culture that they defended had great emancipatory potential for women and the working class. They ran illiteracy campaigns for workers and organized technical/vocational and general cultural courses. They faced

practical problems with initiatives aimed at the creation of free day care in companies and neighborhoods, popular dining rooms, and lecture series, as well as on questions regarding coeducation, sex education, and prostitution.

3. In 1870, Spanish women joined together to create the Association for the Education of Women. This initiative was very controversial, but despite the vehement reactions against it, they consolidated the association and achieved many advances.

4. Without confidence in women's capacities for social transformation, Federica Montseny, the great Spanish anarchist, would have never dedicated her life to politics. She was the spokesperson of CNT (the National Confederation of Workers) and the first woman in Spain to hold office as minister of health and welfare, in 1936–37 (Montseny 1987). During this period abortion was legalized and left to the discretion of the woman.

5. Beck, Giddens, and Lash have named this phenomenon "reflexive modernization," which alludes to the victory that industrial society has had over the reflexive trend of Occidental modernization (1994).

6. In Spain, for example, the feminist symposium held in Granada in May 1979 was the starting point for the important change in the feminist trajectory for modernity. The disenchantment generated by the difficulty of change convinced many women of the need to search for liberation by other means; it was proposed to break with everything and to do something completely different. New forms of feminism began to take over, which proclaimed themselves to be much more specifically attentive to women and their wishes than to the joint struggle for the improvement of all of society. Faced with the tired discussions that do not change anything, new and more creative and feminine formulas had to be found. These formulas broke away from patriarchal plans and resulted in the division of feminism.

7. The *MAR: Women and Contemporary Art* study (CREA 1998–2000) served to verify the critical capacities that nonuniversity women possess to analyze, reflect, and propose the inclusion of women not only as a theme, but as the artists themselves. From the contributions of "other women": (a) we set ways to overcome the elitist barriers that surround the current art world and (b) we worked jointly on didactic materials to improve gender relations through art.

8. Some of their participants take part in a research project coordinated by CREA: *Brudila Calli: The Gypsy Women Against Exclusion* (Instituto de la Mujer). This project aims to overcome the social and economic exclusion suffered by Gypsy women. In this respect, overcoming school absenteeism and failure in school by Gypsy children and teenagers would offer these women an important vehicle of transformation and emancipation, provided by training.

9. This declaration was part of an international project that provided it with a European perspective. The declaration was supported by more than twenty governmental delegations at the 5th UNESCO International Conference on Adult Education.

10. We presented, for the first time, the proposal of dialogic feminism at the conference on *New Critical Perspectives in Education* held in Barcelona in 1994.
11. At the national level in Spain is CONFAPEA, the Confederation of Participants' Associations in Adult Education (with which FACEPA is affiliated). Besides managing both their own associations and projects, the members of the confederation encourage other adults with nonacademic backgrounds to get involved in the definition and management of the various educational projects addressed to them. Its main goal is to create optimum spaces for learning, where there is no coercion or distortion for any cultural, educational, or social reasons.

References

Aixalá, Y. 2000. *Mujeres de Marruecos. Un análisis desde el parentesco y el género.* Barcelona: Ediciones Bellaterra.

Alcoba, E. 2001. De l'art contemporani i la seva difusió. Qüestions de fons. *Temps d'Educació.* Universitat de Barcelona.

Amorós, C. 1997. *Tiempo de feminismo. Sobre feminismo, proyecto ilustrado y postmodernidad.* Madrid: Cátedra.

Arenal, C. 1892. La educación de la mujer. *Boletín de la Institución Libre de Enseñanza,* nº 377. Madrid.

Beck, U., Giddens, A., and Lash, S. 1994. *Reflexive Modernisation: Politics, Tradition and Aesthetics in the Modern Social Order.* Cambridge: Polity Press.

Bourdieu, P. 2000. *La dominación masculina.* Barcelona: Anagrama (original 1998).

Capel, R. M. 1975. *El sufragio femenino en la 2ª. República española.* Granada: Universidad de Granada.

Cooper, D., Faye, J. P., Faye, M. O., Foucault, M., and Zecca, M. 1977. Dialogue sur l'enfermement et la répression psychiatrique. *Change,* 32–33, pp. 76–110. Paris: Collectif Change.

CREA. 1998–2000. *MAR: Mujer y arte contemporáneo.* General Direction XXII. European Direction.

de Botton, L. 2000. *Identidad árabe y mujer desde la igualdad de diferencias.* VIII Conferencia de Sociología de la Educación. Madrid: Universidad Complutense de Madrid.

de Diego, E. 1992. *El andrógino sexuado.* Madrid: Visor

Derrida, J. 1989. *De la Gramatología.* Madrid: Siglo XXI (original 1967).

Fagoaga, C. 1985. *La voz y el voto de las mujeres. El sufragismo en España 1877–1931.* Barcelona: Icaria.

Flecha, R. 2000. *Sharing Words: Theory and Practice of Dialogic Learning.* Lanham, Md: Rowan & Littlefield Publishers.

Flecha, R., Gómez, J., and Puigvert, L. 2001. *Teoría Sociológica Contemporánea*. Barcelona: Paidós.

Foucault, M. 1992. *Vigilar y castigar*. Madrid: Siglo XXI (original 1975).

Giddens, A. 2000. *On the Edge: Living with Global Capitalism*. London: Jonathan Cape.

Giddens, A. 1993. *The Transformation of Intimacy: Sexuality, Love and Eroticism in Modern Societies*. Cambridge: Polity Press.

Giroux, H., and Flecha, R. 1992. *Igualdad Educativa y Diferencia Cultural*. Barcelona: El Roure.

Habermas, J. 1984. *The Theory of Communicative Action*. Boston: Beacon Press (original 1981).

Habermas, J. 1987. *The Philosophical Discourse of Modernity: Twelve Lectures*. Cambridge, Mass: MIT Press (original 1985).

Habermas, J. 1996. *Between Facts and Norms: Contribution to a Discourse Theory of Law and Democracy*. Cambridge, Mass: MIT Press (original 1992).

Habermas, J. 1998. *The Inclusion of the Other: Studies in Political Theory*. Cambridge, Mass: MIT Press (original 1996).

hooks, b. 1989. *Talking Black. Thinking feminist, Thinking Black*. Boston: South End Press.

Humm, M. (ed.). 1992. *Feminisms. A Reader*. London: Harvester Wheatsheaf.

Irigaray, L. 1994. *Thinking the Difference: For a Peaceful Revolution*. New York: Routledge.

Jackson, S. (ed.). 1993. *Women's Studies. A Reader*. London: Harvester Wheatsheaf.

Leroux-Dhuys, J. F. 1998. *Les abbayes cisterciennes en France et en Europe*. Paris: Place des Victoires.

Lyotard, J. F. 1984. *La condición postmoderna*. Madrid: Cátedra (original 1979).

Mernissi, F. 1993. *El poder olvidado. Las mujeres ante un Islam en cambio*. Barcelona: Edic. Icaria-Antrazyt.

Montseny, F. 1987. *Mis primeros cuarenta años*. Barcelona: Plaza & Janes ed.

Nicholson, L. (ed.). 1997. *Second Wave: A Reader in Feminist Theory*. New York: Routledge.

Nicholson, L. 1999. *The Play of Reason: From the Modern to the Postmodern*. Ithaca, NY: Cornell University Press.

Puigvert, L., et al. 2000. Mujer popular y educación de personas adultas. *Trijornadas en Educación democrática de personas adultas*. July 7, 8, pp. 135–141. Barcelona: El Roure.

Puigvert, L. 2001. *Las otras mujeres*. Barcelona: El Roure.

Rorty, R. 1989. *Contingence, Irony and Solidarity*. Cambridge: Cambridge University Press.

Sánchez, M. 1999. La Verneda–St. Martí: school where people dare to dream. *Harvard Educational Review*, vol. 69. No. 3, pp. 320–335.

Valcárcel, A. (comp.). 1994. *El concepto de Igualdad*. Madrid: Pablo Iglesias.

Young, I. M. 1997. *Intersecting Voices: Dilemmas of Gender, Political Philosophy, and Policy*. New Jersey: Princeton University Press.

Young, I. M. 2000. *Inclusion and Democracy*. Oxford: Oxford University Press.

Housework-Migrant Women and Marriage-Migrant Women: Women in a Globalizing World

※※※

Worldwide Population Movements

Over the last few decades, geographic mobility has rapidly increased all over the world. More and more people are covering great distances, beyond the boundaries of their region of origin and, inevitably, over national borders as well. Above all, among the causes of such movements we find flight and expulsion, as a result of the violence that is unleashed by ethnic and national conflicts, along with poverty and hunger, and the inequalities between the economies of the First and Third Worlds.

These causes are not enough to explain the increase in worldwide migratory shifts. There has always been poverty, hunger, flight, and expulsion. What then is different about now? Today, and this is the key point, they are happening in a new context, the context of globalization, characterized by the reduction of time and space. Technological development has contributed to this process by facilitating a rapid expansion of opportunities for mass transport and mass communication (from incredibly cheap travel and charter flights to videos, satellite TV, and the Internet). The more this kind of infrastructure grows, the easier and faster the distances are spanned. While economic globalization is strengthened and promoted, processes of transnationalization of labor and capital adopt various forms, from the spread of transnational businesses to the emergence of transnational elites. As a consequence, new means and forms of looking for work beyond local, regional, and national borders are at the reach of a growing number of people. Flexibility and mobility are the imperatives that arise in the new world economy. At the same time, the process of globalization facilitates any enterprise. Whereas in the past one had to be something of an adventurer to go abroad, nowadays there are well-trodden paths and routes for this, keeping in mind the networks and communities of the people who left their place of origin earlier on.

The Mass Media as a Driving Force behind Transnational Life Plans

Above all, mobility requires a readiness to mobilize oneself. The idea of tempting one's fate and taking on a journey to new ports is not inherently logical. So, why does the idea find such wide acceptance and carry so much resonance these days? Evidently the many opportunities presented by cultural globalization play a major role by feeding people's fantasies with its new messages, incentives, and motivations. The Indian anthropologist Arjun Appadurai analyzed the enormous influence of mass media like film, television, and the news. Their wide circulation reaches all continents and distant lands, where they are no longer confined to the big cities, but find their way into the remotest villages, be it in India or in East Anatolia. Oftentimes these media transmit a distorted image of reality, full of fiction and myth.

Whether they depict reality or not, the decisive element that Appadurai makes abundantly clear is that these images today influence the life plans and expectations of a growing number of people in an increasing number of places in the world. More persons throughout the world see their lives through the prisms of the possible lives offered by mass media in all their forms. That is, fantasy is now a social practice; it enters, in a host of ways, into the fabrication of social lives for many people in many societies.[1]

Instead of simply conceiving of life as destiny, more and more people are beginning to imagine other worlds and to compare them with their own. So life for the ordinary person is no longer determined just by the immediate situation but increasingly by the possibilities that the media (either directly or indirectly) suggest.[2]

To put it another way: Why should I kill myself working to

continue being poor, exploited, hungry, and desperate if in other places there are people who live in freedom, well-being, and dignity, who have enough to eat, a house, and a car, and can visit the doctor when they are ill? Why not try to go there?

Cultural globalization, along with economics, contributes to the spiral of geographic mobility. In the process of confluence in which they mutually reinforce each other, they feed the migratory processes that characterize our present times: Increasingly more people leave their homeland to try their luck and find a future in some distant promised land.

A Look at Women Migrants

The Anglo-Indian author Hanif Kureishi adeptly captured the situation by stating that the immigrant was the Everyman of the twentieth century.[3] His statement is valid not only for the twentieth century but also for the twenty-first, for both men and women. Women migrants make up a growing population; this is the group I shall focus on here. I will inquire into factors such as opportunities, hopes, and privations, which characterize the lives of migrant women.

What do we actually know about women migrants? It is not surprising that in the 1990s there was a report published by the United Nations Secretariat in which international female migrants were referred to as "the invisible half,"[4] pointing to the fact that up until then existing research on migration had focused on men. Recently the situation has changed a bit. Gradually women migrants have come to the fore in politics, in science, and in society in general. In what follows, I'll discuss two groups that are gaining greater significance but about which we still know very little: migrant women domestic workers and migrants by reason of marriage.

Domestic Work Migrants

After the devastation caused by the Second World War, many Western countries in the fifties and sixties experienced a period of great economic upsurge. These expanding economies urgently needed a labor force, and when it could not be found inside the country, it was brought in from outside; many people left their economically weak homelands to find work and better living conditions in more industrialized countries. Most of them, mainly men,[5] did unskilled jobs or work whose skills were taught in the workplace. There is a considerable amount of research and documentation about this form of labor migration in Germany as well as internationally.

More or less from the 1980s, we have been witnessing a new kind of labor migration. There are women from Mexico working in California as nannies, women from the Philippines looking after the elderly in Israel, and Polish women doing the cleaning and washing and ironing in German homes—all of these women have found work in the domestic arena. Although as of yet there are few relevant studies on this theme, there is no doubt about the following: For the most part, those who carry out this kind of work are women, many of whom, despite having qualifications, have very meager hopes of securing a steady income in their own country due to the economic situation. A recent study provides the following figures:

> Before they migrated from the Philippines to the USA and Italy, the Filipina domestic workers in Parrena's study had averaged $176 a month—often as teachers, nurses and administrative and clerical workers. But by doing less skilled (though not easier) work as nannies and maids and care service workers, they can earn $200 a month in Singapore, $410 in Hong Kong, $700 a month in Italy and $1,400 a month in Los Angeles.[6]

But why is it that this form of labor migration by female domestic workers has become increasingly more significant in recent years? The first reason is clear, given that it is the one that triggered the earlier waves of labor migration: the disparity between poor and rich countries. But unlike the fifties and sixties, today the more industrialized countries no longer look for unskilled labor. Economic crises and restructuring have affected many sectors of industry. An increasing number of companies are adopting "rationalization plans," which basically means a reduction of personnel and, as a result, the disappearance of many jobs, especially in the sectors that employed migrant workers.

In addition we must not forget the changes in the political map of Europe. With the collapse of communism, many jobs formerly subsidized by the state that can no longer be financed in the new situation have been eliminated. In Russia, Ukraine, and eastern Europe, a growing number of people now have to cope with unemployment and the uncertainty of not knowing how they will provide for their families.

But the way out of these difficulties available in earlier decades—industrial jobs in the West—is no longer there. The jobs can now be found in its private households. We will look at this solution now in greater detail.

Relieving the Strain for Some Women

I'll begin by looking at the so-called traditional division of labor, that is, the one that gradually developed in bourgeois families in the eighteenth and nineteenth centuries, where the husband was the one who supported and fed the family, while the wife in essence ensured that "all the husband's energy was devoted to his job."[7] Given that paid work did not include any other spheres of life, the wife assumed most of the everyday tasks that the husband was not responsible for. It is precisely that kind of paid work that I refer to as "one-and-a-half-person" jobs: Remunerative work tacitly presumed that the working person could call on the aid of other people. This in most cases meant the wife. Since she did not have (or had only in a very restricted form) remunerative work, she remained unseen in the background from the standpoint of salaried occupation. As a result, this "background occupation" directly benefited salaried work.[8]

The traditional model continues to be in vigor, but times have changed. In Western society, in Europe and North America, many young women are no longer prepared to devote all of their energy and commitment to advancing their husband's career. On the contrary, they are qualified and motivated to get and maintain their own paid job.

The question is how this can be done while the conditions of the "one and a half person" still exist. Men in the younger generations tend to take on more of the share of family duties than their fathers or grandfathers did. But as empirical studies show time and again, an equal division of labor in the private sphere is still a long way off.[9] It is evident that there is an "ideological emancipation"[10] among men, but the change and support in daily practice are oftentimes quite lacking. In the words of Arlie Hochschild, the result is an "unfinished social revolution"[11] that will continue to be a problem for many women.

The solution, at least for now, and to the extent that it is possible, lies in new ways of labor division among women. In the rural areas and the lower social strata, it has been defined, at least until now, as a generational distribution (the grandmothers care for the grandchildren). Meanwhile, in the urban middle class there is an increased trend based on geographic mobility that is directly related to social inequality. Part of the domestic tasks are delegated to foreign women who have no opportunities for getting a job in the official labor market since they have no work experience or proficiency in the language, e.g., Turkish cleaning women and Bosnian nannies working in Germany. The sociologist Maria S. Rerrich has analyzed how this pattern manifests itself:

> On the one hand the German social welfare state is based on an erroneous premise, which considers women with families who have an occupation to be an exception. This intrinsically patriarchal misconception in our society results in a considerable workload in the daily lives of millions of working women. It obligates them to urgently seek individual solutions to relieve themselves of these burdens insofar as they can afford it. On the other hand there is a state integration policy, which is set up in such a way that many foreign women can only find work offered in the informal sector in private households. Supply and demand run parallel in the sphere of reproduction, such that the structural needs of two different groups of women coincide. The conclusion is that without a political solution, the "one-and-a-half person" jobs will become "one-and-a-half class" and "one-and-a-half nation" jobs in the future.[12]

So it seems very possible that in the future, more types of these private international connections will form. With the fall of the borders between the European east and west, with the approximation of the poor and rich nations (impervious to even a restrictive isolationist policy), the rich Western countries will have a strong power of attraction. While these countries lack the public infrastructure that allows women equal participation in the labor market, women will be forced to find survival strategies and solve their needs using private mechanisms. In light of the panorama that this incomplete social revolution offers, women from poorer countries will increasingly turn to a significant market for the labor of women in Germany, the United States, France, Italy, etc.

Under these international conditions, the traditional division of labor breaks down in the complex relations between the First and Third Worlds. No longer is it companies and the industries that absorb immigrant workers—families also accept a growing number of women originating from other countries. In a time of radical political change and complex migratory movements, the international division of labor is on our very doorsteps, so much so that it is entering our homes.

This goes for my own family too. My uncle, an art historian and highly intellectual, is now 91 years old and gravely affected by Alzheimer's disease. He is cared for at home around the clock by two young Polish women. Of course I'm glad that he has this care, but at the same time I am concerned about the situation of the two young Polish women, one of whom has a husband and children at home in Poland. What will become of them?

Shedding the Burden but at What Price?

This anecdote about my own family is not at all atypical. As far as we know from the few existing studies, the population of migrant domestic workers is heterogeneous. Many, especially the young and single women, left for financial motives, but also from a curiosity, seeking adventure and the possibility of seeing a new part of the world. Even if it meant being away for only a few months, it helped them leave their homes.[13] Many left their countries with their families, oftentimes as a consequence of war or expulsion, and are now working to make a bit more money to live in their new land.[14] On the other hand, others left behind husband and children and now try to make money in the new country, the wealthier one, to send back home so that their families can live in better conditions there.[15]

This last group is the women who live between "here" and "there." They are the transnational migrants in the strictest sense of the term. While in earlier decades it was the men who made up the pattern of transnational migration, today more and more women are on the scene. In both cases the consequences are very similar.

Physical proximity, coexistence, and face-to-face relationships are some of the defining characteristics of the family in its traditional sense. Considerable separation in terms of time and space between women and their husbands, mothers and children, brothers and sisters, are defining traits of the transnational migratory currents articulated and limited institutionally. Oftentimes family relationships adopt new configurations. The shape and meaning of what is known as the "family" must be redefined and reinterpreted. Traditionally it was taken as a given that where there is "love," families should remain together. But now, in the globalized world, we find that the opposite situation prevails: The person who loves his or her family is ready to leave it behind or arrange it in various different ways in order to seek conditions for a better future in another location.

Upon a closer look, it is evident that the consequences are different based on whether it is a man or a woman who goes to another country. According to the traditional view, the woman is responsible for household tasks and looking after the children. If the woman, or mother, is responsible for these tasks, then how is it that she has to work abroad? If women are working in other countries caring for other families, elderly, and children, what will happen to their own family?

In this situation there arises what Arlie Hochschild calls "global care chains," which are characterized by a series of personal links between people across the globe based on paid or unpaid work of caregiving. Global chains usually start in a poor country and end in a rich one. But some such chains start in poor countries and move from rural to urban areas within that same poor country.[16] A caregiving chain might take the following form: The eldest daughter of a family in the Second or Third World looks after her younger brothers and sisters while her mother, a migrant worker, works as a nanny looking after another woman's children in a rich Western country. Another example can be found in a study that is currently being carried out in Germany, which shows how women from Poland go to Germany as domestic workers, while Ukrainian women travel to Poland to relieve these migrant domestic workers in their homes.[17]

There are new forms of motherhood emerging from this situation—specifically, variations that can be called transnational mothering. They involve relinquishing expectations that we take for granted. Even though our society today is increasingly prepared to accept a plurality of mothering arrangements—

whether they involve single mothers, working mothers, stay-at-home mothers, lesbian mothers, surrogate mothers, and so on—we still take as a given, even in feminist debates, that mothers live with their children and that their relationship takes place in a shared space. Globalization is bringing about radical changes in this context as well. In a study of Latin American migrants, Pierrette Hondagneu-Sotelo and Ernestine Avila conclude:

> Transnational mothering situations disrupt the notion of family in one place and break distinctively with . . . the "epoxy glue" view of motherhood. Latina transnational mothers are improvising new mothering arrangements that are borne out of women's financial struggles, played out in a new global arena, to provide the best future for themselves and their children.[18]

These new forms of transnational mothering are predominantly the result of economic pressures and are not based on the free choice of women. The migrant women workers interviewed by Hondagneu-Sotelo and Avila repeatedly spoke about the pain and longing that life away from home brought up.[19] Thus, the new form of labor migration has two faces. On the one hand it provides a life free of hunger and poverty, but at a considerable cost to women and their families.

Marriage Migrants

Another one of the consequences of migratory movements is that, in Germany as in other countries, there has been an increase in the number of marriages in which the members of the couple are of different nationalities.[20] In many of these marriages, we find numerous examples of unions in which there is a

TABLE 1. Foreign spouses of German men, according to the country of origin

1987		1999	
Philippines	1303	Poland	5304
Yugoslavia	1207	Russia	2223
Austria	1045	Thailand	2148
Poland	977	Romania	1592
Thailand	853	Ukraine	1436

Source: Federal Statistics Office (Statistisches Bundesamt)

TABLE 2.   Foreign spouses of German women,
according to the country of origin

1987		1999	
USA	2831	Turkey	3971
Italy	2131	Yugoslavia	3314
Turkey	1477	Italy	2005
Austria	1159	USA	1254
Great Britain	1068	Austria	931

Source: Federal Statistics Office (Statistisches Bundesamt)

significant disparity between the economic situation of the
country of origin of the husband and of the wife. Some clear examples of this are marriages of a US man with a Russian woman,
a German man with a Thai woman, or an Australian man with a
Filipino woman. In the case of Germany, the data in the tables
point to a clear preference by German men for women from the
Far East and eastern Europe, while, among German women, note
the sudden appearance of Yugoslavian men.

Victimizers and Victims

Generally, we see that men oftentimes marry women from countries with economic problems, that are politically unstable or in
a process of modernization that is stagnant. For this reason these
types of unions attract attention from the media and the public.
Also, we cannot overlook the activities of marriage agencies,
which offer these types of unions as their service. We often read
announcements such as these published in the press:[21]

Goodbye to overemancipation!
Charming Ladies from Poland, Russia, Eastern Germany.

An exclusive and very special foreign marriage bureau!
Hungary—Bulgaria—Romania—South America
Loyal, beautiful, loving women
No complicated procedures—quick introductions

International Marriages Arranged
We organize introductions to affectionate, loyal, home-loving
women, with refined manners from St. Petersburg

(German- or English-speaking).
Favorable conditions. Individual attention and
arrangements for a successful outcome.
Interesting Video Interviews.

Attractive Russian women proficient in German and English,
all heart and soul for the man and the family. Secretaries,
Interpreters, Academics, seeking serious life partners.

Women from Bohemia, German-speaking, attractive,
demure and very family-oriented, are looking
for eligible males to marry.
All you need to do is send us details of your age,
occupation, your family situation, and your address.
We reply by means of a plain envelope.

Statistics, magazine articles, and newspaper accounts do not
paint the men in a favorable light. Stories of violence and abuse
complete the picture. It all leads us to conclude that we are deal-
ing with men who are incapable of maintaining a healthy relationship, who are socially inept, and opposed to female emancipation. The perception is that Western women are too independent
for their liking, and they seek a woman who they presume has a
weaker cultural disposition and economic position, who is less
demanding and more compliant. In the event that the woman
does not fulfill his expectations, he can use his power against her
by beating her, confining her, or sending her back to her home
country. In short, the man becomes an unbearable companion,
an oppressor, and the woman is a helpless victim.

Maybe at this point I should confess that I too interpreted and
ascribed such portrayals as behaviors resulting from gender.[22] But
with time I have become more cautious. Where have my doubts
come from?

Analyzing the Sources

The Advertisements for Marriage

Let's assume that the professional marriage agencies that adver-
tise in the newspapers have correctly gauged the wishes of their

clientele and that the advertisements provide us some indication of the type of men who use their services. The gist is that they generally have difficulties maintaining a normal social life.[23] But we cannot generalize and talk about "all men"; instead we must specify that we are speaking about a concrete group of men who are attracted by these kinds of offers. We cannot glean anything at all from the advertisements with regard to the motives that other men have for entering binational marriages.

Reports in the Media

Newspapers have to provide what their readership finds interesting. Oftentimes the articles that attract the attention of the public are those that look at individual cases that are sensational, exotic, and dramatic. In the more reliable media there is often an attempt to situate the story in a sociopolitical context and bring the issue to light and help the victim, especially when the victim is a woman (it is no coincidence that there are many women filmmakers or women journalists who report on wives from poor countries and their partners). In any case, we see how different motives lead to similar final choices. They end up presenting the public with the relationships that are fairly uncommon and generally tend to be less happy than the average. There is a tendency to show stories that are out of the ordinary that end up reinforcing the stereotypes of feminine and masculine roles, in which the man is seen as the violent oppressor and the woman as helpless and weak. There is no doubt that these situations exist, and of course they must urgently be exposed. The question is, just how typical are they? And what image of reality do they create in public opinion?

Scientific Research

The majority of existing studies about the situation in Germany are strongly focused on practical measures and on resolving [24] problems. Most of them are commissioned by political institutions with explicit objectives of tackling crime, especially crimes against women. These studies analyze prostitution, trafficking of people, and the marriage trade in the same way. The sample is also predefined in function of the objective. Those who turn to resource centers for women are interviewed, as well as the social workers who attend them. Police reports, affidavits, and documents from legal proceedings are used as additional and complementary materials for the research. Of course this is necessary if we want to trace irregular situations. But if we want to know about the world beyond these irregularities, we can be sure that this is not the way to find out. If we interview women who turn to women's centers of some kind, we will inevitably encounter women who have problems that they are unable to resolve on their own. Those who analyze police complaints and court proceedings will undoubtedly find little more than offenses and criminals. This is not news to anyone. But not every man with a wife from Russia, Poland, or Thailand is a wrongdoer, just as not every woman from these countries who marries will end up in a women's center seeking help. How many people does this apply to? The answer is, we just don't know.

There is no question that there is a need for studies of the dark side of binational unions. But because of their limited and unidirectional scope and the fact that they speak only on a superficial level about the fact that not all women experience violence and oppression, the image that remains in the end is shallow, incomplete, and distorted. The fact that the studies are focused on irregularities contributes to promoting the idea that the deviancies analyzed in the studies characterize the norm. Titles like "Experiences of Women Migrant Workers" or "The Myth and the Reality of the Bicultural Marriage Market"[25] contribute to perpetuating this image, although they address very specific groups of migrant women and a very particular marriage market. This difference is not plain for all readers. At least it has been difficult for my students to realize this; it was a challenge for them to leave behind the widespread prejudice that the marriage of a German man with a Polish or Russian or Thai wife is synonymous with violence, oppression, and exploitation.

From a Different Perspective

That which is expressed above appears surprisingly evident in other studies. Take for example a research investigation[26] on Filipino women who immigrated to Australia through unions organized by the marriage trade. Unlike earlier studies, this one does not look solely at women, but has a much broader scope and is more equipped to unravel the complexity and heterogeneity of these types of relationships. The final conclusion appears much more balanced and, in fact, more positive. Firstly, the study includes an introduction to the background: "Undoubtedly, some exploitation and certain illegal practices are associated with this type of migration. However, it should be remembered that there is a long tradition in Australia of seeking out single women for immigration with a view to providing wives for Australian men."[27] And then we are warned explicitly about false stereotypes: "One must guard against stereotyping the causes and consequences of the phenomenon. . . . While exploitation of some Filipino women undoubtedly occurs, that is by no means the norm . . . many of the marriages of Filipino women and Australian men are happy and mutually rewarding."[28]

A small study[29] carried out in Germany about women who emigrated from the ex–Soviet Union to marry and who now live in Berlin is based on a wider sample that includes "marriages for love" and "marriages of interest." This study, as well, includes a background that is objective and undramatic: "Individual and voluntary migration for purposes of marriage is one of the oldest and most continual forms of migration from the Soviet Union." The study takes into account "the great competence of women," who do not appear as victims but as "subjects" who knowingly take part in the migration process.[30] It illustrates clearly that the relationship between marriage and migration cannot be reduced to a simple framework and depicted in a negative light; rather, we are witnesses to a "very broad spectrum of life plans."[31]

We reiterate that the studies oriented toward resolving problems are necessary. It's undeniable that within the constellation of the relationships between men from the First World and women from the Second or Third World, politico-social forces are significant, especially those that refer to the imbalances within relationships of power and unilateral dependence. From the standpoints of economic security, linguistic competence, social contacts, and permits for residency and work, there is no question that the man has the advantage by living in his own country. All of this is so without telling us much about how this type of relationship actually unfolds in each particular case, or the factors that contribute to its failure or success. It becomes clear that we must broaden the perspective with regard to analyzing this type of relationship, which would simultaneously benefit the women in question. Therefore, we must ask the following: What are the social, historical, and legal conditions that might help to attain the "dream of a better life,"[36] which moves so many women to choose emigrating for marriage? When does it end up being a tragic nightmare? When does it turn into a bearable or even happy life?

Other Hopes

I have deliberately chosen the expression "bearable." In the studies that are oriented toward resolving problems, there are formulas that surprised me. Women researchers note repeatedly—without hiding a certain annoyance—that many of the female migrants interviewed are somehow finding ways of resolving difficulties in their marriages. The women migrants develop "relatively pragmatic behaviors" vis-à-vis marriage problems, ignoring many things, like their personal expectations with regard to their husband, as long as they have a basic agreement.[33] The conclusion is that "women adopt a strategy of resignation in their relationships, which makes the marriage more bearable and provides them with an apparent happiness on a functional level."[34]

Note the term "apparent happiness." Is it really only "apparent"? We should know the circumstances in more detail, but this seems to be the general conclusion. It could be that the migrants have given up all hope, but it also might be that they are flexible or resilient enough to adjust their expectations (which themselves may have been flawed from the beginning)—a premise that does not seem so outlandish at all. We must look for answers in what we already know about the motivations of migrant women,[35] from which we can infer that what they want above all else is to escape the difficult economic and social conditions of their homeland. Even when they have qualifications for employment in their own country, it is challenging to get a job that allows them to make a decent living, due to the problematic situation in the labor market there. Their husbands are also unemployed or earn very little, so that marriage, which has been the traditional solution for women, offers no financial security either. To all of this we must add other situations that further complicate women's abilities to get by. In countries like Thailand, where virginity is a feminine obligation, it is impossible for many women, especially for mothers, to find a serious relationship. How can they fulfill the cultural tradition that dictates devotion and respect toward their family, which includes providing financial support to their parents and their siblings? Women have numerous obligations but at the same time few prospects of satisfying them. The Western husband appears as one of the few possibilities in reach. In the words of a Brazilian migrant woman: "When I met him, I thought, I'm going. . . . He is my future. . . . He is my opportunity. I shall go to Germany."[36] There is no place for romanticism or personal joy, for sweet sentiments or bliss. Love is good, and if someone can actually find it, she is lucky. But what women really look for is much more practical and earthly—a way out of misery.

If these are their expectations, can we really say that they have resigned themselves, that their happiness is only feigned? Or is it another kind of happiness, which we have to measure by a relative standard? This is the key question. We cannot really answer it by means of existing publications. But we can at least be mindful of a recurring problem when we, women researchers in the West, approach women from other cultural realities and make them the objects of our studies based on our own perspectives. For we must not only learn to inquire about what we have in common as women from our own point of view, but also learn to take into account the differences between them and us. Otherwise we project our cultural values and conceptions of the world onto them—for example, our Western ideal of the happy family and relationship, or our individual life plans. In this way we will never be able to find out what motivates other women, what their hopes and expectations are, and what for them constitutes a happy life.

Conclusion

We live in a time when gender roles have indeed changed, but only to the extent of an "unfinished social revolution." Another determining characteristic of our time is progressive worldwide globalization, in which national frontiers appear more permeable and it becomes increasingly more common for people to leave their country of origin either voluntarily or driven by circumstances, in order to build a future elsewhere.

These two trends together produce radical changes. To investigate them we must focus on the new social inequalities that exist today. These do not only involve the imbalances between "more developed" regions and "less developed" regions; we must also include the inequalities between women from one region to another, and consequently, between the families of the women from the different groups. As Hochschild writes with regard to women migrant domestic workers: "Globalization may be increasing inequities not simply in access to money, important as that is, but in access to care."[37]

On the other hand, we, women researchers from the First World, must consciously endeavor to approach women from the other worlds with caution and respect. This is how I understand the basic principle of dialogic feminism. We cannot approach other women from a position of wanting to "help" them so much, which is always tainted with a certain kind of condescending, know-it-all attitude. Instead we must learn to see the complexities of their world, without reducing it to black-and-white images, and take notice of the distinctiveness of their life projects.

In many regions of the world today, women are replacing the typical male migrant worker. Women migrants find work precisely because they can be discriminated against, but they use the new circumstances in their lives in order to change their personal situation. And something similar happens in the case of women who migrate for marriage. They enter a situation of extreme inequality with regard to power and dependence, and it is not just a few who pay a high personal price for it. However, they are not just passive victims, but also women of action, who build and orient their lives according to *their* values, standards, and ideals.

It is not always easy for Western researchers to understand this, precisely because we believe in "sisterhood." Culturally mixed couples not infrequently experience something similar— couples with different skin colors, religions, or nationalities who followed the powerful call of "love" might find that their partner suddenly seems surprising, unpredictable, and even annoying.[38] What goes for these couples also goes for women researchers who seek points of connection with women from other worlds. The objective must not be to erase the differences, for that would be impossible anyway. Instead, it is a case of accepting the differences, recognizing them, and living with them. The "challenge of living with differences" continues to be the task.[39]

Notes

1. Arjun Appadurai (1991), Global ethnoscapes: notes and queries for a
   transnational anthropology. In: Richard G. Fox (ed.), *Recapturing
   Anthropology: Working in the Present*. Santa Fe, New Mexico: School
   of American Research Press, p. 198.
2. Appadurai 1991, p. 200. In the original: "Ordinary lives together are increasingly powered not by the givenness of things but by the possibilities that the media (either directly or indirectly) suggest are available."
3. Hanif Kureishi (1990), *The Buddha of Suburbia*. London, Boston: Faber
   and Faber, p. 141.
4. United Nations Secretariat (1995). The international migration of
   women: an overview. In: United Nations (ed.), *International Migration
   Policies and the Status of Female Migrants*. New York: United Nations
   Publications, p. 1.
5. In Germany, for example, the proportion of women employees taken on
   as *Gastarbeiter* [guest workers] was 20%. See: Martina Schöttes and
   Annette Treibel (1997), Frauen—Flucht—Migration. Wanderangsmo-
   tive von Frauen und Aufnahmesituationen in Deutschland. In: Ludger
   Pries (ed.), *Transnationale Emigration*. Soziale Welt, Sonderband 12.
   Baden-Baden: Nomos, p. 104.
6. Arlie Passell Hochschild (2000), Global care chains and emotional sur-
   plus value. In: Will Hutton and Anthony Giddens (eds.), *On the Edge.
   Living with Global Capitalism*. London: Jonathan Cape. Also: Simone
   Odierna (2000), *Die heimliche Rückkehr der Dienstmädchen. Bezahlte
   Arbeit im privaten Haushalt*. Opladen: Leskie und Budrich, p. 147ff.
7. Cynthia Fuchs Epstein (1971), *Woman's Place. Options and Limits in
   Professional Careers*. Berkeley and Los Angeles: University of California Press, p. 115.
8. Elisabeth Beck-Gernsheim (1980), *Des halbierte Leben, Männerwelt
   Beruf, Frauenwelt Familie*. Frankfurt: Fischer, p. 68.
9. See, for example, Manfred Garhammer (1997), Familiale und gesells-
   chaftliche Arbeitsteilung—ein europäischer Vergleich. In: *Zeitschrift
   für Familienforschung*, year 9, vol. 1, pp. 28–70.
10. Klaus Schneewind et al. (1992), *Optionen der Labansgeztaltung junger
    Ehen und Kinderwunsch*. Stuttgart: Kohlhammer, p. 237.
11. Arlie Hochschild in collaboration with Anne von Machung (1990), *Der
    48-Stunden-Tag. Wege aus dem Dilemma berufstätiger Eltern*. Wien,
    Darmstadt: Paul Zsolnay, p. 34ff.
12. Maria S. Rerrich (1993), Auf dem Weg zu einer neuen internationalen
    Arbeitsteilung der Frauen in Europa? Beharrungs- und Verände-
    rungstendenzen in der Verteilung von Reproduktionsarbeit. In:
    *Lebensverhältnisse und soziale Konflikte im neuen Europa. Verhand-
    lungen des 26 Deutschen Soziologentages in Düsseldorf 1992*. Frank-
    furt: Campus, pp. 93–102; on p. 100.
13. See, for example, Bill Jordan et al. (1997), Leben und Arbeiten ohne
    regulären Aufenthaltsstatus. Brasilianische Migrantinnen in London
    und Berlin. In: Hartmut Häussermann and Ingrid Oswald (eds.), *Zu-*

wanderung und Stadtentwicklung. Leviathan, Sonderheft 17. Opladen: Westdeutscher Verlag, pp. 215–231.

14. See Odierna 2000, p. 147ff.

15. See Hochschild 2000; also Pierrette Hondagneu-Sotelo and Ernestine Avila (1997), "I'm here, but I'm there": The meanings of Latina transnational motherhood. In: *Gender & Society,* year 2/vol. 5, pp. 548–571.

16. Hochschild 2000, p. 131.

17. Maria S. Rerrich, oral evidence from a current research project on migrant domestic workers.

18. Hondagneu-Sotelo/Avila 1997, p. 567.

19. Idem, e.g., pp. 49, 554.

20. Data about Germany from 1995 show that in that year, people who married in the Federal Republic were almost always German. Only in 1 out of every 25 marriages was the partner a foreigner (the phrase used in the official statistics is "Ausländerinnen oder Ausländer beteiligt"); that is, at least one of the partners was a foreign passport holder. See Statistisches Bundesamt (ed.) (1995), *Im Blickpunkt: Ausländische Bevölkerung in Deutschland,* Stuttgart: Metzler Poeschel, p. 26; the figures refer to western Germany. In 1999, by contrast, 1 in 6 marriages was "von oder mit Ausländern," that is, the husband or the wife or both were foreign nationals (my own computation using figures in Statistisches Bundesamt [1995], Fachserie 1, Reihe 1, 1999: "Eheschliessungen nach der Staatsangehörigkeit der Ehepartner" [unpublished draft]); again, the figure refers to western Germany.

21. Source: *Süddeutsche Zeitung,* August–October 1992.

22. Elisabeth Beck-Gernsheim (1995), Mobilitätsleistungen und Mobilitätsbarrieren von Frauen. Perspektiven der Arbeitsmarktentwicklung im neuen Europa. In: *Berliner Journal für Soziologie,* vol. 2, pp. 163–172.

23. Dagner Heine-Wiedemann et al. (1992), *Umfeld und Ausmass des Menschenhandels mit ausländischen Mädchen und Frauen. Schriftenreihe des Bundesministers für Frauen und Jugend* [a series of booklets produced by the Federal Minister for Women and Youth], vol. 8. Stuttgart: Kohlhammer, p. 124ff.

24. Heine-Wiedemann et al. 1992 ; Ilse Lenz et al. (1993), *Internationaler Frauenhandel. Eine Untersuchung über Prostitution und Heiratshandel in Nordrhein-Westfalen und die Interventionsmöglichkeiten von Institutionen und Frauengruppen.* Published by the Ministerium für die Gleichstellung von Frau und Mann of the Land of Nordrhein-Westfalen. Düsseldorf 1997; see also Elvira Niesner et al. (1997), *Ein Traum vom besseren Leben. Migrantinnenerfahrungen, soziale Unterstützung und neue Strategien gegen Frauenhandel.* Opladen: Leske und Budrich; Elvira Niesner (2000): Mythos und Wirklichkeit auf einem bikulturellen Heiratsmarkt. In: Ellen Freiden-Blum et al. (eds.), *Wer ist fremd? Ethnische Herkunft, Familie und Gesellschafft.* Opladen: Leske und Budrich, pp. 163–181.

25. Niesner et al. 1997, Niesner 2000.

26. Graeme Hugo (1995), Migration of Asian women to Australia. In: United Nations (ed.), *International Migration Policies and the Status of*

Female Migrants. New York: United Nations Publications, pp. 192–220.

27. Idem, p. 202.

28. Idem, p. 204.

29. Stephan Beetz and Tsypylma Darieva (1997), "Ich heirate nicht nur den Mann, sondern auch das Land." Heiratsmigrantinnen aus der ehemaligen Sowjetunion in Berlin. In Häussermann and Oswald (eds.), *Zuwanderung and Stadtentwicklung*, op. cit., pp. 386–405.

30. Idem, pp. 386–387.

31. Idem, p. 403.

32. Niesner et al. 1997.

33. Niesner 2000, p. 179.

34. Niesner et al. 1997, p. 44.

35. Niesner et al. 1997, p. 28; Niesner 2000, p. 167; Hiene-Wiedemann et al. 1992, p. 135.

36. Quoted in Niesner et al. 1997, p. 28.

37. Hochschild 2000, p. 142.

38. Elisabeth Beck-Gernsheim (2001), Ferne Nähe, nahe Ferne. Überraschungseffekte in binationalen Familien. In: *Zeitschrift für Familiendynamik*, year 26, vol. 1, pp. 4–21.

39. Susan Weidman Schneider (1989), *Intermarriage: The Challenge of Living with Differences Between Christians and Jews*. New York: Free Press.

Transformative Encounters

I was pleased and surprised to receive Lídia Puigvert's first contribution to this exchange. I was pleased because her commitment to a dialogic version of feminism seems important, if not indispensable, to any feminist account of social transformation. But I was surprised because the essay implicitly addresses one who would call herself a postmodernist, or would defend the position of postmodernism. And I thought to myself: Perhaps they have invited the wrong person to be an interlocutor for Lídia's view because I cannot recognize myself in the terms that are provided here. Perhaps I am suffering from paranoia, and she does not actually understand me as one of those postmodernists. But I know from experience that this term comes up in relation to me; it is always used by others to describe me, and it is always used not to defend the political relevance of my work, but to dispute it. So, on the one hand, I am pleased to have this chance to open up an international dialogue and to discuss so many issues that commonly concern us: e.g., feminist theory and the task of social transformation, the politics of inclusion, radically democratic and inclusive social movements. On the other hand, I have some worry, because if a dialogue is to work—if the persons who enter into dialogue are to learn from one another and, indeed, be transformed by one another—then it is important not only that each know her own convictions but also how to listen to the other's voice, to read the other's words, to live patiently with the convictions and passions that motivate the other in her daily life and her various modes of self-expression.

I would even argue that one of the greatest needs that all individuals have, which has been more or less systematically denied to women, is the need for recognition. No concept of dialogic feminism can proceed without that concept. But let us think for a moment about what recognition means, and what it entails. My understanding, in part conditioned by Hegel, is that we do not present ready-made selves to one another; we do not encounter the other and then simply present or re-present what is already true about us, what is already constituted in us, what is already known about us. In the encounter with the other, we are perhaps always somewhat strange to ourselves, for the other addresses us in ways that make assumptions about who we are, what we stand for, what the limits of our thinking and commitments might be. But if we undergo the experience of dialogue, then we enter the conversation as one kind of person but emerge as another kind. This is simply to say that the best kind of dialogue is that which offers the possibility for each participant to be transformed through the process itself. Indeed, why would I have come to Barcelona if I did not want the chance to be transformed by what I encounter here?—not only to learn from the voices of others, but to experience those voices in their embodiment, their life, the context of their struggle, and to have my own voice, in the effort to speak to you here across languages, transformed by virtue of "you" being the ones I address.

Lídia's paper seems to me to have two concerns: The first is to make sure that academic feminists listen to women who are not part of academia, to women who are part of a larger movement of women who are seeking conditions of equality and making demands for greater inclusion in participatory politics. The second is to have us all realize that the project of modernity is the one which will ensure that we can and will engage in a meaningful project of social transformation. There are two opponents in her paper. The one is a group of academic feminists who are elitist and do not listen to, and are not transformed by, the voices of women outside of academia, especially poor women and women who are engaged in fundamental struggles. The second opponent is postmodernists. They are said to annul the capacity for social transformation, to reject the value of the subject, to debunk principles of reason and claims of universality.

And here is where I am stymied by the problem of address, since I am not sure whose work and what positions fall into these various categories. And because we have only a characterization of these positions, but no reading, no engagement with the texts of lectures of those who are said to hold these positions, we do not know whether what Lídia says about them is true. I am wondering whether dialogue can happen if we do not take seriously the words of the other. I am wondering whether democracy is possible, whether a feminist movement which works across the lines of class and literacy and culture is possible, without learning how to pay attention to the words that others offer, to find what they are saying in and through them. These seem to be aspects of "dialogic feminism," so I am at a loss to understand what kind of dialogue is possible when characterizations take the place of an attentive listening or engagement. Surely, this is not what modernity would have us do.

For the record, let me try to state my view, a view which is not mine alone, but which has in effect been developed through a sustained encounter between social movements—feminist, anti-racist, anti-imperialist—and a movement within academia. I do not know what "postmodernism" is, only that it has some meanings in architecture and art and that it has others within the realm of social theory. I do not subscribe to it, not do I know enough about what it is to accept it or deny it. In fact, I have never understood what people mean when they use this term. They bunch together a group of thinkers who are very often very different from one another, if not fully incompatible. I know of no one who says that she does not believe in human agency, or that he will have nothing to do with reason or with claims of universality. Is it really true that people argue on these bases? I do not think so.

But there is some kind of debate, and in this sense Lídia's paper is trying to communicate something important. She wants us to accept that "modernity" is the rubric under which social transformation can occur and that, as feminists, we should also identify as modernists. Now, if I say that I am neither a modernist nor a postmodernist, I am afraid that this will be taken as a sure sign of my postmodernism. But perhaps I am simply asking for us to change the terms of the debate. My view is that there are various ways of understanding "modernity," which are not always compatible with one another, and that it is not even necessarily what we mean by "modernism" in art and literature. I find it interesting that Lídia's view of modernity has a European historical basis, and that it does not tell us whether modernity was experienced differentially by the poor and the rich, by property owners and those emerging from bonded labor. Many scholars these days ask "Whose modernity?"—whether, for instance, diasporic Africans have already experienced modernity or are presently experiencing it, or are experiencing it in the same way that Europeans have told the story of their modernity. When we consider that the parameters of Europe are usually uncontested in the "coherent" narratives of modernity we receive, that the architects of modernity, such as Hegel and Spengler, understood the "subject" to be a European man, a colonialist, one whose sense of "place" and forward trajectory was incontestable, as incontestable as the march of European colonialism itself, then we are surely right to question whether modernity has a gender (and if so, which one?) and whether it makes assumptions about colonial power and keeps that power in place. If we are committed to a radically inclusive democratic vision of feminist politics, we must interrogate the concept of modernity, not to deny or dispute it, but to see which of its resources are useful to us in our contemporary struggles, and which are not.

So, I think it would be honest and true to say (and here I am pleased to speak in the language of "truth" and without embarrassment) that it is important to sustain a critical relation to modernity. This is not to say that I am for it or against it. But it is a call for a change in the terms of the debate. A democratic project of any kind must always sustain a *critical* relation to the terms which provide a framework for thinking. Now, to sustain a critical relation to the term "modernity" is not the same as *being* a modernist or a postmodernist; it is to ask about the distinction, to see how it operates, to seek to know, in an open-minded way, what is at stake when people use the term to say what is necessary—what it connotes, what is connoted in contrast to it, what it cannot be.

In the United States, there were and are several different ways of questioning the category of "the subject." But to question the category is not to do away with it. And it is not to deny its usefulness, or even its necessity. But to question the subject is to put at risk what we know, and to do it not for the thrill of the risk, but because we have already been put into question as subjects. We have already, as women, been severely doubted: Do our words carry meaning? Are we capable of consent? Is our reasoning functioning like that of men? Are we part of the universalist community of humankind? Gloria Anzaldua, in her work *Borderlands/La Frontera,* writes in both Spanish and English, as well as in American Indian dialects, and compels her reader to read all of these languages as they attempt to read her book. She clearly crosses the border between academic and nonacademic writing and, to emphasize the value of living on the border, lives as a border in relation to an array of different cultural projects. She says that in order to have social transformation, one must get beyond a unitary subject. She is in favor of social transformation, has struggled for it her whole life, and has taught in the university. Do we say that she belongs to the group called "academic" feminists? Well, it would be ridiculous to exclude her from that group. Her work is read in academia. She sometimes teaches at the University of California. She is active in different movements, especially for Latin American women, who suffer in the United States from lack of health care and exploitation within the labor market, and often struggle with immigration issues as well. Do we say that she is one of the "other women" who is outside of academia? Well, it would be foolish to exclude her from that group as well. When she says, for instance, that she is not a unitary subject, that she does not accept the binary oppositions of modernity, she is saying that she is defined by her very capacity to cross borders—as a chicana, for instance, one who was compelled to cross the border from Mexico to the United States, who returns to that border to write her fiction, who struggles with the complex mix of cultural traditions and formations which constitute her for what she is: chicana, Mexican, lesbian, American, academic, poor, writer, activist. Do all of these strands come together in a unified way, or does she live their incommensurability and simultaneity as the very meaning of her identity, an identity culturally staged and produced by the very complex historical circumstances of her life?

So, for instance, what do we do with the border crossers? The women who are perhaps both in academia and in movements, who spend part of their time studying and reading and part of their time struggling as activists? And what do we make of those who engage in activism within the university, trying to make room for women's studies, for research on women, who helped to establish CREA itself? Is that not political work? Is that not activism? Does it help us or hurt us to conceive of "other women" as those who do not read or attend school or the university? And where do we think we all come from? If we are academics, that does not mean we did not grow up poor, or that our families are not still poor, perhaps illiterate. Anzaldua asks us to consider that the source of our capacity for social transformation is to be found precisely in our capacity to mediate between worlds, to engage in cultural translation, and to undergo, through the experience of language and community, the diverse set of cultural connections which make us who we are. One could say that for her, the subject is "multiple" rather than unitary, and that would get the point, in a way. But I think her point is more radical. She is asking us to stay at the edge of what we know, to put our own epistemological certainties into question, and, through that risk and that openness to another way of knowing and living in the world, to expand our capacity to imagine the human, and to be able to work in coalitions across difference, which will make a more inclusive movement. What she is arguing, then, is that it is only through existing in the mode of translation, constant translation, that we stand a chance of producing a multicultural understanding of women or, indeed, of society. The unitary subject is the one who knows already what she is, who exits the conversation the same as when she entered, who fails to put her own epistemological certainties at risk in the encounter with the other, and so stays in place, guards her place, becomes an emblem for property and territory, *refusing self-transformation, ironically, in the name of the subject.*

Gayatri Chakravorty Spivak has a similar view, although she has said that whereas Anzaldua maintains a notion of a multiple subject, she has a notion of a fractured subject. Indeed, her view is that we cannot appreciate the oppression that women of color have experienced within the global political and economic framework of First World imperialism without realizing that "women" as a unitary category cannot hold, cannot describe, that it must undergo crisis and expose its fractures to public discourse. She asks, time and again throughout her work, what does it mean not only to listen to the voices of the disenfranchised, but to "represent" those voices in one's work? On the one hand, it is possible to treat the disenfranchised as if they were voiceless and to appoint oneself as their voice. I think we saw this, quite problematically, when the American feminist Catharine MacKinnon announced at the Vienna Human Rights Forum that she "represented the women of Bosnia." Perhaps she thought that the women of Bosnia were voiceless, but she certainly learned otherwise when they made plain their clear public opposition to her effort to appropriate and colonize their position.

Given the history of the missionary—of colonial expansion which supposedly takes place in the name of cultivation, modernity, progress, and enlightenment, "the white man's burden"— feminists as well must ask whether the "representation" of the poor, the indigenous, and the radically disenfranchised within academia is a patronizing and colonizing effort, or whether it seeks to avow the conditions of translation that make representation possible: to avow the power and privilege of the intellectual along with the links in history and culture which make an encounter between poverty, for instance, and academic writing possible. Spivak translates the work of Mahasweta Devi, a fiction writer who is also an activist, whose work now, thanks to Spivak, appears in academia, at least the English-speaking one. Devi writes as a South Asian tribal woman, and for and about tribal women. And so her voice comes to me through a translation, a translation offered by Spivak, in which I am asked to respond to, and to take responsibility for, a world in which these voices are not only to be represented, but to be part of a vision of collective transformation. Spivak insists that the writing of Devi cannot be called simply "tribal" or made to represent the "tribal," because in this writing there is also, and by way of the tribal, a vision of internationality at stake. In Devi's stories, women suffer in part because the land is exploited and ravished, because the traditional means of working are systematically being destroyed by developers. In this sense, it is a local story. But those developers are also linked to broader currents in global capital. As Spivak puts it, "A strong connection, indeed a complicity, between the bourgeoisie of the Third World and migrants in the First cannot be ignored" (198).

If we read Devi closely, we see that she is making connections, living connections, between the tribal and the global, and that she is herself, as an author, a medium of transit between them. She is clear that the possibilities of long-term global survival and radical environmental politics and of nonviolence as a political practice depend not on a disembodied "reason," but on elaborating the sense of the sacred. Spivak thus writes, "Large-scale mind change is hardly ever possible on grounds of reason alone. In order to mobilize for non-violence, for example, one relies, how-ever remotely, on building up a conviction of the "sacredness" of human life" (199). Spivak also accords Devi the name of philoso-pher and offers the following advice for radical thinking and acti-vism: "I have no doubt that we must *learn* to learn from the origi-nal ecological philosophers of the world, through the slow, attentive, mind-changing (on both sides), ethical singularity that deserves the name of "love"—to supplement necessary collec-tive efforts to change laws, modes of production, systems of edu-cation, and health care. This for me is the lesson of Mahasweta [Devi], activist/journalist and writer" (201).

For Spivak, the subaltern woman activist has been excluded from the parameters of the Western "subject" and the historical trajectory of modernity. That means that for the most part the tribal woman is a spectator to historical advance. Similarly, if we consider the traditions of Afro-Caribbean writing, we can ask as well whether this body of writing is within the traditions of mod-ernity or whether it is, always and in different ways, comment-ing on what it is to live "outside of history."

So it should be clear that I think a critical relation to moder-nity is necessary. But do we know whether we can do without the resource of modernity? To answer this question, let me con-sider another position, that of Paul Gilroy, a British sociologist and cultural studies researcher, whose book *The Black Atlantic* has made a profound impact on both African American and di-asporic studies in the last five years. His work is of importance to feminists precisely because we may at once be wary of the lega-cies of modernity and want to make use of some of the ideals and principles that have been articulated within the frameworks of modernity.

The first ninety pages of that book are concerned with the He-gelian notion of modernity. He argues there that the exclusion of people of African descent from European modernity is not a suffi-cient reason to reject that modernity, for the terms of modernity have been and still can be appropriated from their exclusionary Eurocentrism and made to operate in the service of a more inclu-sive democracy. At stake in his subtle historiography is the ques-tion of whether the conditions of reciprocal recognition by which the "human" comes into being can be extended beyond the geopolitical sphere presumed by the discourse of equality and reciprocity. And though Hegel gives us the strange scene of the lord and bondsman, a scene which vacillates between a description of serfdom and slavery, it is not until the work of W. E. B. Du Bois, Orlando Patterson, and Paul Gilroy that we start to understand how the Hegelian project of reciprocal recognition might be renarrated from the history of slavery and its diasporic effects.

Gilroy argues that the perspective of slavery "requires a discrete view not just of the dynamics of power and domination in plantation societies dedicated to the pursuit of commercial profit but of such central categories of the Enlightenment project as the idea of universality, the fixity of meaning, the coherence of the subject, and, of course, the foundational ethnocentrism in which these have all tended to be anchored" (55). Less predictably, Gilroy then argues that it would be a great mistake to dismiss the project of modernity. Citing Habermas, he notes that even those who have been most radically excluded from the European project of modernity have been able to appropriate essential concepts from the theoretical arsenal of modernity to fight for their rightful inclusion in the process. "A concept of modernity worth its salt," he writes, "ought, for example, to have something to contribute to an analysis of how the particular varieties of radicalism articulated through the revolts of enslaved people made selective use of the ideologies of the western Age of Revolution and then flowed into social movements of an anticolonial and decidedly anticapitalist type" (44).

Gilroy takes issue with what he calls postmodern forms of skepticism that lead to a full-scale rejection of the key terms of modernity and, in his view, a paralysis of political will. But he then also takes his distance from Habermas, noting that Habermas fails to take into account the relationship between slavery and modernity. Habermas' failure, he notes, can be attributed to his preference for Kant over Hegel. Gilroy writes, "Habermas does not follow Hegel in arguing that slavery is itself a modernizing force in that it leads both master and servant first to self-consciousness and then to disillusion, forcing both to confront the unhappy realization that the true, the good, and the beautiful do not have a shared origin" (50).

Gilroy proceeds to read the writings of Frederick Douglass, for instance, as "lord and bondsman in a black idiom" and then to read the contemporary black feminist theorist Patricia Hill Collins as seeking to extend the Hegelian project into that of a racialized epistemology. In these and other instances, he insists that the Eurocentric discourse has been taken up profitably by those who were traditionally excluded from its terms, and that the subsequent revision carries radical consequences for the rethinking of modernity in nonethnocentric terms. Gilroy's fierce opposition to forms of black essentialism, most specifically Afrocentrism, makes this point from another angle.

One of the most interesting philosophical consequences of Gilroy's work is that he provides a cultural and historical perspective on current debates in philosophy that threaten to displace its terms. Whereas he rejects the hyperrationalism of the Habermasian project, even as he preserves certain key features of its description of the Enlightenment project, he also rejects forms of skepticism that reduce all political positioning to rhetorical gesture. The form of cultural reading he provides attends to the rhetorical dimension of all sorts of cultural texts and labors under the aegis of a more radically democratic modernity. Thus, his, I would suggest, is a position worth considering as one rehearses the debates between the defenders and the detractors of the Enlightenment project. It shows us that we do not have to choose between untenable alternatives, that is, between a hyperrationalism, which presumes to know in advance what all communication requires, and a hyperrelativism or skepticism, which leads us to believe in the impossibility of all value claims. Indeed, we might say, with some confidence, that the task for contemporary politics is precisely to find one's way between a cultural imperialism which thinks it knows in advance, prior to any encounter, what it will take to find common ground with others, and a point of view which assumes in advance that all efforts to communicate will end in aporia (or a dead end).

I finished this essay three days after the terrorist attacks on the World Trade Center and the Pentagon in September 2001, attacks which were brutal and devastating, and which raised questions of international politics, nonviolence, and transformative encounters. Most Americans probably experienced something like the loss of their First Worldism through this event. The United States was supposed to be the place which was not attacked, where life was safe from violence initiated from abroad, where the only violence we knew was the kind that we inflicted upon ourselves. But we saw that the national borders were more permeable than we had thought. There were those who took the occasion to rethink and criticize US imperialism, to ask about the violence we inflicted on other countries, in what ways we helped to dispossess Arabs, how our support for Israeli war tactics came back to haunt us. But most people did not react that way. Instead, there was hysterical racism and strong bipartisan support for the suspension of civil liberties and for the "manly" retaliatory strike, or war, which has reinstituted the masculine character of the nation and overcome its perceived castration, through a cycle of violence in which manhood itself is constantly at stake. The United States is no victim. It claims that the violence against it is itself a declaration of war, but if that is true, then the violence that the United States has been promulgating abroad has been a long and repeated declaration of war. It remains to be seen whether the United States can realize that the violence which has come back to haunt it is part of a cyclical pattern it has fostered and developed. Through the terrorist attacks, we have a chance to see that our foreign policy—for instance, the systematic dispossession of the native peoples of Palestine—has consequences, and that the United States, by virtue of its power and its geographical distance, is not therefore immune to the consequences of its own violence. One can root out terrorists, but if one does not alter the practices which constitute the systemic conditions for terrorism, one will not stop the cycle of violence itself. And if the United States cannot avow its own terrorism, it will be subject to its return again and again.

Women clearly have a voice to make heard here, since violence has never been far from us. Will there be a public discourse, for instance, on the question of how a collective deals, ultimately, with its vulnerability to violence? Women know this question well, have known it in nearly all times, and nothing about the advent of capitalism made our exposure to violence any less clear. There is the possibility of appearing impermeable, of repudiating vulnerability itself. There is the possibility of becoming violent ourselves. But perhaps there is some other way to live such that one is neither affectively dead nor violent. And that has to do with demanding a world in which bodily vulnerability is protected without therefore being eradicated, since vulnerability is also a strength: the source of our openness to others, which finally permits of a transformative encounter.

Consider that the struggle for recognition requires that each partner of the exchange recognize not only that the other needs and deserves recognition, but that we are each, in different ways, compelled by the same need, the same requirement. This means that we are not separate identities in the struggle for recognition, but already involved in a reciprocal exchange, an exchange which dislocates us from our positions, our subject-positions, and allows us to see that community itself requires the recognition that we are all, in different ways, striving for recognition. When we ask another for recognition for ourselves, we are not asking for that other to see us as we are, as we have always been, as we were prior to the encounter. Rather, in the asking, we are already becoming something new, since we are avowing a connection with the other, a need and desire for acknowledgment by the other, without which we could not be. This means that recognition does not freeze us in our place, our position, our various locations, but rather compels us to move beyond what we have been and to encounter a new possibility for collective exchange.

The Italian philosopher Adriana Cavarero writes that I cannot tell my own story without a "you," without a "you" to whom I address myself, because "I" come into being only on the condition of the "you." What Cavarero tells us in her book *Relating Narratives: Storytelling and Selfhood* is that the encounter between the "I" and the "you" does not resolve easily into a "we," and that contemporary political movements are mistaken to override the irreducibility of this encounter through the assertion of a collective "we." For Cavarero, the question to ask is not "what" we are, as if the task were simply to fill in the content. But the question to be asked of the other is a direct one: "Who are you?" And this question assumes that there is some "other" there, whom we do not know and cannot fully apprehend, and whose uniqueness and nonsubstitutability sets a limit to the model of reciprocal recognition offered within the Hegelian scheme. Making use of Arendt and Levinas, Cavarero argues that we are beings who are of necessity exposed to one another, and that our political situation consists in how to handle this constant and necessary exposure. I am not, as it were, an interior subject, closed upon myself, solipsistic. I exist in an important sense for you, and by virtue of you. If I have lost the conditions of address, I have lost "myself."

> The "you" comes before the "we," before the plural "you" and before the "they." Symptomatically, the "you" is a term that is not at home in modern and contemporary developments of ethics and politics. The

"you" is ignored by individualistic doctrines, which are too preoccu-
pied with praising the rights of the "I," and the "you" is masked by a
Kantian form of ethics that is only capable of staging an "I" that addresses itself as a familiar "you." Neither does the "you" find a home
in the schools of thought to which individualism is opposed—these
schools reveal themselves for the most part to be affected by a moralistic vice, which, in order to avoid falling into the decadence of the
"I," avoids the contiguity of the "you" and privileges collective, plural
pronouns. Indeed, many revolutionary movements (which range from
traditional communism to the feminism of sisterhood) seem to share
a curious linguistic code based on the intrinsic morality of pronouns.
The "we" is always positive, the plural "you" is a possible ally, the
"they" has the face of an antagonist, the "I" is unseemly, and the
"you" is, of course, superfluous. (90–91)

So there are two points to be made here: The first has to do with
our fundamental dependency on the other, the fact that we cannot
exist without addressing the other, without in some ways being
addressed by the other, and that there is no wishing away our fundamental sociality. The second, however, limits the first point.
No matter how much we each desire recognition and require it,
we are not therefore precisely the same as the other—there is an
irreducibility to our being, one which becomes clear in the distinct stories we have to tell, which means that we are never fully
identified with any collective "we." The way that Cavarero puts
it, "What we have called an altruistic ethics of relation does not
support empathy, identification, or confusions. Rather this ethic
desires a *you* that is truly an other, in her uniqueness and distinction. No matter how much you are similar and consonant, says
this ethic, your story is never my story. No matter how much the
larger traits of our life-stories are similar, I still do not recognize
myself *in* you and, even less, in the collective *we*" (92). The
uniqueness of the other is exposed to me, but mine is also exposed
to her, and this does not mean we are the same, but only that we
are bound to one another in our singularity.

⊗⊗⊗

I confess to not knowing whether what I have just laid out is
modernist or postmodernist. And I presume I will be forgiven if I
continue not to know and, finally, not to care. I do feel strongly,
though, that the question of an encounter, a transformative one, is
crucial to what we are engaged in here, and that it is a question, a

concern, that not only crosses the divide between academic and nonacademic feminism, but in some ways is the very question that is posed to that divide. Do we really think that we must decide on a common methodology before we can march in the street together? I doubt it. I think that we could have several engaged intellectual debates going on at the same time and find ourselves joined in the fight against violence. I think we could disagree on modernity and find ourselves joined in asserting and defending the rights of indigenous women to health care, reproductive technology, decent wages, physical protection, cultural rights, freedom of assembly. And if you saw me on such a protest line, would you wonder how a postmodernist was able to muster the necessary "agency" to get there? I doubt it. The fact is that various routes lead us into politics; various stories, reasonings, and beliefs bring us into the street, and we do not need to ground ourselves in a single model of communication, reason, or notion of "the subject" before we are able to act. Indeed, an international coalition of feminist activists and thinkers, which affirms the thinking of activists and the activism of thinkers and refuses to put them each into distinct categories which deny the actual complexity of the lives in question, will have to be one which accepts an array of sometimes incommensurable epistemological and political beliefs which bring us into activism. There will be differences among women—for instance, on what the role of reason is in contemporary politics: Spivak insists that it is not reason which politicizes South Asian tribal women suffering exploitation by capitalist firms, but a set of values and a sense of the sacred which comes through religion. And Cavarero claims that it is not by virtue of the fact that we are reasoning beings that we are connected to one another, but by virtue of the fact that we are exposed to one another, requiring a recognition which does not substitute the recognizer for the recognized. Do we want to say that it is our status as subjects which bind us all together when for many of us the subject is multiple or fractured? And does not the insistence on the subject as the precondition of political agency erase the more fundamental modes of dependency which bind us, out of which our thinking and caring emerge, the basis of our vulnerability and our resistance?

My sense is that when we ask what allows us to encounter one another, or what the conditions are for the possibility of an international feminist coalition, we cannot look to the nature of "man" or the a priori conditions of language, or the timeless conditions of communication. We have to consider the demands of cultural translation which are imposed upon us as we think about the global dilemmas that women face. It is not possible to impose a language of "rights" developed within First World contexts on women who are facing the threat of imperialist economic exploitation and cultural erasure. We know that the language of rights can work to justify colonial expansionism. This does not mean that we should avoid or refuse to use the language of rights. But it does mean that the "rights" discourses which are developed have to be done at the grassroots level, with reference to the global context, and that this dual consciousness will belong to those who are living both contexts at once, shuttling between them, whose lives depend upon the success of cultural translation itself.

Similarly, I think it is both necessary and good to speak of "universal" rights, or to speak of political participation as that which should be universally inclusive. This is an important discourse, one which has huge effects on local, national, and international political bodies and without which we would be politically paralyzed. But we would be making a mistake if we thought we understood already which rights, and which formulation of rights, are and are not universal, which groups are and are not included within the universal, which meaning for "universality" we should agree upon. The point is that we are still in the process of articulating what conditions of universal enfranchisement and equality might be. This is not quite the same as saying that the project of modernity is unfinished—because what I am saying is that the project of modernity is unfinishable; as the project is appropriated in various contexts and for various reasons, it is unclear that it is still "modernity" that is at issue. When rights are declared to be "universal," this is an abstract claim. And though there may be rights on the books which are declared to be universal, we know that they are not realized concretely in many lives. We see this, for instance, when people are deprived of food, shelter, home, work, when they are forcibly separated from family and community, when forced emigration leaves them landless and stateless, exposed to state terror and economic exploitation. When we ask what it will take to help a stateless people achieve protection, entitlement, and guarantees of freedoms within a democratic regime, or to regain secure title to land that belongs to them, we are constantly confronted with a question of which rights, whose rights, articulated how, and backed up by what power? And how much of political mobilization is and should be about the status of "rights"? When and where do we ask the question of how we want to live together? It may be that "rights" will be one thing we want to have secure in that vision of living together, but I do not think we want to understand ourselves fundamentally or exclusively as rights-bearing citizens. How fundamental is the discourse of rights to the discourse of politics?

Most of our international discourse centers on questions of rights, but how much of it centers on trying to acknowledge and bring into the political arena the concrete dilemmas of what it is to be local and global at once, to be caught in the necessity of constant translation, and what kind of bind this is. Such an inquiry neither moves too quickly to assert our commonality, thus effacing our difference, nor seeks to return us to our parochial locations, our ethnic singularities, without showing how the most local struggles are implicated in the processes of globalization. What this also means is that the usual binary oppositions do not hold, and that we must learn to work with one another in our irreducible complexity, bound to one another in many ways, implicated in a process of globalization which works differentially and relentlessly, at the same time that we are irreducible to a collective condition.

When one considers the strategies of the Zapatista movement in Mexico, one sees this situation perhaps in a dramatic way. They are clearly modern, making use of technology and disseminating their cause through the Internet, but they also insist on their folklore—on disseminating the myth, for instance, that Votàn-Zapata lives. In this sense, according to José Rabasa, the movement exemplifies the "compatibility of modern and non-modern cultural and political practices" (399). But the Zapatista movement also, clearly, engages in a discourse of human rights and self-determination, which it knows will be refuted, refused, and ridiculed. There is no possibility of seeking recourse to a common set of presuppositions about human beings, to the demand for dignity or recognition, which every human deserves, since their language is not considered communicable by the government. In Rabasa, one of the Zapatista participants in the 1995 consultations with the government explains this experience of the uselessness of communication:

They [the government] also told us that they were studying in depth what dignity is, that they are doing research and studies on dignity. What they could understand above all was that dignity was service to others. And they asked us to tell them what dignity means to us. We answered that they should go on with their research. It makes us laugh, and we laughed in their faces. (414)

The Zapatistas make their demands for justice, democracy, and liberty to the government, but they understand as well that only the demise of the government will bring about the realization of their demands. As a result, they cannot achieve a solution through dialogue with a partner whose very legitimacy within the dialogue is not accepted. As a result, the claims that are made are addressed to an other, but they are impossible claims, and the other who would hear them, honor them, does not exist. The mode of address is thus utopian in the sense that it seeks to call forth an other who might honor their demands. But communication under these circumstances with those who are fundamentally committed to not recognizing them is impossible. Rabasa and others argue that this very impossibility of communication is what constitutes the radicalism of this politics, and what gives it its sense of radical hope. That the government can stand by principles of "dignity" while it systematically destroys the conditions for a dignified life for the Zapatistas shows us in clear terms that the universality of such matters as human dignity cannot be taken for granted, even when it is earnestly defended by those who destroy it. Clearly, the discourse of dignity cannot save the Zapatistas in this instance, but the laughter seems crucial. It marks the limits of communication, the task for translation, the place where a nonencounter emerges in the place of a collective or mutual recognition. When one calls for recognition, one must always ask, from whom? and within which terms? The one who might confer it may well be illegitimate, and the terms within which it is conferred may well work to one's disadvantage.

This is not a reason to give up the struggle for recognition, but only a reason to consider what might qualify as a legitimate and hopeful scenario for its occurrence. Recognition cannot lock us in place if it is to belong in a radical democratic politics. It must release us into an open future, one in which, having come up against the limits of our knowing, we might finally apprehend what is different and become other than what we know, in which our encounter with the other proves essential to our own well-being and sense of futurity. In this sense, then, we must seek a *transformation* through recognition rather than the guarantee of our demise or, indeed, anyone else's.

References

Gayatri Chakravorty Spivak. 1993. *Imaginary Maps.* New York: Routledge.

Gloria Anzaldua. 1991. *Borderlands/La Frontera.* San Francisco: Spinster's Ink Press.

Adriana Cavarero. 2000. *Relating Narratives: Storytelling and Selfhood.* London: Routledge. (Translated from the Italian)

José Rabasa. 1997. "Of Zapatismo: Reflections on the Folkloric and the Impossible in a Subaltern Insurrection," in Lisa Lowe and David Lloyd, eds., *The Politics of Culture in the Shadow of Capital.* Durham, North Carolina: Duke University Press.

Equality of Differences

I read Judith's first chapter with an interest that surpassed the high expectations with which I anticipated it. I consider *Gender Trouble* of great importance for the development of gender studies, and *Bodies That Matter* as a continuation of this intellectual work. Its contribution to queer theory, which is widely recognized, reevaluates the contributions that gay and lesbian groups are making in different fields of thought. The agility of her writing, dressed with fabulous metaphors and with titles as suggestive as *Antigone's Claim*, rediscovers implications in words that have passed unperceived.

With these precedents, it is logical that I anticipated her chapter with interest. Her interpretation surprised me because its content specifies her previous contributions in such a way as to point toward very interesting theoretical lines for the future. Above all, I share her vision of the transformative role that theoretical works must play, along with social and political interventions that aim to contribute to the improvement of social reality.

In this transformative task we share, I would like to highlight the importance of universal values, in which human rights for all people are established. I was particularly interested in her distancing herself from some postmodern positions that, on the basis of securing a radical relativism, question the legitimacy of human rights. Her critique of norms does not exclude the need to judge criminal acts or to establish rights that all people must have. She proposes a reflection about norms in which the human does not exclude her existence in the end, but opens it up to future change. The incorporation of the undetermined nature of concepts such as "gender" and the "human" constitutes an independent variable that makes such concepts flexible to present and future reconceptualizations. Thus, we can use these concepts as political strategies toward social transformation. Without a doubt, the defense of a "project of discourse" and "international politics" about human rights, which includes "local perceptions of what is human" would surprise many people who have been lacking, till present, a translation of Judith Butler's work.

An optimal understanding of these concepts would allow us to refine the conditions of their practical and social use. This must be our guide in the fight for transformation, which must take place as a dialogue between all the voices involved whenever improvements for all women are proposed. This includes those of us who work in universities in privileged countries, as well as the "cleaning women" in these countries and women doing agricultural work in non-Western countries. I see that Judith's text supports this perspective as well as, with a few differences, the works of Habermas, which she accurately cites. In the following text, my approach will be from this point of view.

A perception of social dynamics based solely on claims of power reduces relations between people to relationships of domination, and in this way makes relative the legitimacy of transforming them. In order to alter these dynamics, we need to have dialogic practices that include the voices of all who are involved. Dialogic feminism is profoundly transformative, given that it demands and secures egalitarian social conditions that allow for dialogue to take place. This dialogue can be practiced only when we, as subjects, assume the social and personal responsibilities that our reflections and actions imply, and when we are open to changing our theoretical positions according to valid arguments. Social and personal transformation should go hand in hand. In this sense, the dialogue established with Judith during the meetings has led me to revise some of the things that I had previously written. Although we come from different theoretical orientations, we are both fighting to open up new perspectives toward social transformation for women, accepting a dialogue that is also open to many others.

The way I view gender studies today is inseparably linked with the ongoing dialogue and collaboration that I maintain with the "other women." They demonstrate that the academic sphere does not have exclusive capacity to articulate valid proposals for overcoming specific social problems concerning women. In what follows, I will attempt to incorporate into the debate with Judith certain reflections that my work with them has brought me to.

I begin with a dialogue between a feminist academic and a "traditional housewife," introduced in a chapter in Flecha 2000. The former (Laia) wants to make the latter (Chelo), who rejects feminism, aware of her need to be liberated. Gradually, the dialogue leads Laia to begin to see that her model of liberation, in many aspects, is not what she had thought, being that it is not valid for every woman's situation. At the same time, Chelo accepts the fact that some of her ideas could be formulated from another perspective, such as that of a feminism that considers the plurality of the voices of all women:

> Laia and Chelo disagreed on many points, but they were spontaneously united in the feminist struggle for equal educational rights. (. . .) To be a faithful "wife" like Chelo was different, not better nor worse, than to be a liberated woman like Laia. The subject-object distinction of traditional modernism made no sense; no one had the right to consider herself the subject who should impose her will on the other, reducing her to a simple object. An even worse choice was to dissolve the subject, proposing that each individual should do whatever she could or whatever she wanted, thereby converting the egalitarian principles into false arguments to be destroyed or claiming that nothing is blameworthy, not even rape or abuse at home or on the street. Intersubjectivity, on the other hand, respects the options resulting from dialogue and rejects those imposed through violence. (72–73)

In my reflection on Laia and Chelo, I am particularly interested in how a truly intersubjective dialogue (is there any other kind?) dispenses with validating arguments based on the "prestige" of the speaker. A reflection on the concepts that guide feminism, from whose urgency Butler's work arises, can acquire new dimensions if the debate incorporates all women's perspectives and eliminates any elements that challenge dialogue and inhibit the setting out of proposals. The social transformations in gender relations (in which women's movements have had a significant role) have reached a point where now we can propose to overcome not only the traditional categories of masculinity and femininity, but also those of different types of femininity, such as the "liberated feminist" (Laia) and the "housewife" (Chelo).

Butler brings us to a consideration of heterosexuality not only as a sexual choice, but also as the normative apparatus of a worldview that constrains life in two ways: It defines what is normal and excludes what is not normal. Through this prism, we see the genesis of a binary thought, in which "good" and "bad," "active" and "passive," "health" and "illness," etc., constitute mechanisms that organize reality into hierarchies; sexual difference itself is part of heterosexual theory, which—according to Butler—has pervaded the feminist movement. This situation could be overcome with the establishment of new dimensions within the categories of the discourse that lead to looser boundaries. Thus, she indicates the urgency of signaling and establishing a new approach to concepts that articulate feminist theory, and with it, gender relations. Butler shows that gender violence is manifested in an especially virulent manner when these dichotomies have been transgressed and their universal legitimacy and natural character called into question. The artificiality of the symbolic order constructed about sexual difference on the whole is made evident, thus throwing the status quo into crisis. Being a man and looking like a woman, or vice versa, constitutes a serious questioning of the immobility of the established categories, and can become part of a political proposal that makes these categories more flexible.

I agree with Judith on the fundamentals with respect to the need for transforming the categories of identity that have guided gender relations, avoiding the essentialism that makes us its victims. With the construction of identity, gender categories, and norms, people must yield to a heterosexual and binary hegemony. Nevertheless, I would like to point to dialogue and reflection as ways of opening these categories, avoiding certain problems about identity inherent in the discourse of Foucauldian theory, which on many occasions portrays itself as an alternative. If we based our arguments on Foucault, we would have to use a notion of identity that is reduced to "identity discourse," which domesticates the individual, imposing on him notions such as "normality" or "abnormality." On a theoretical level, challenging traditional identity would be part of a current critique of the tendency in Western metaphysics to reduce people to substances (in premodernity/pre-Enlightenment) and subjects (in modernity). On a more concrete level, we could say that this challenge does not quite assume the capacity to change the identities, norms, responsibilities, and social rights that people can exercise.

Foucault's genealogical perspective assumes that identity is established with regard to that which is considered normal, resulting from the power structure, a limitation on our capacity for action, therefore, it is something to be challenged. In light of this, we can point out that the demands made by different social groups have been articulated in terms of some common characteristics considered to be features of identity. Here we must ask ourselves, as women, whether the gender norms that constitute our identity are a burden that we must get rid of, to gain more freedom, or whether we can use these norms, through reflection, to construct a society in which the plural does not exclude, but complements; in which we are not victims but architects of the norms—which are always in process—governing the relations between the genders. Let us also say that reflection itself should be an open category, flexible and resulting from dialogue between different possibilities that benefit one another. In this way, the other is not defined as a comparison, but as a complement.

In addition, I consider that Foucault's vision, inherited from Nietzsche and Bataille, does not help to propose positive alternatives to surmounting the inequalities between men and women. In the first place, yielding the birth of values to the spheres of power delegitimizes any valuable platform from which to arrive at agreements that move beyond a succession of relations of submission. The very agreement would be experienced only as an imposition. Secondly, if people's real freedom consists in resistance to such impositions, then transgression is justified not just as the consequence of an end, but as an end in itself. Thus, "sexual freedom" should not be limited by submission to any type of restrictions; it already deals with norms and consent.

MICHEL FOUCAULT: We can always have the theoretical discourse that consists of saying: At any rate, sexuality cannot in any case be penalized. And when rape is penalized, only the physical violence should be punished. [One could] say that it is no more than an aggression, and nothing else: whether someone puts [his] fist in someone's mouth or [his] penis in someone's vagina, there is no difference. . . . But, in the first place, I am not sure that women would be in agreement.

MARINE ZECCA: Not at all, no. No way.

MICHEL FOUCAULT: So admit that there is an offense that is "solely sexual."

MARINE ZECCA: Ah, yes.

MARIE ODILE FAYE: For all the girls who have been assaulted in a public park or in the subway, all of those experiences of daily life, at eight, ten, twelve years old: very traumatic . . . (Cooper, Faye, et al. 1977: 32–33)

When Chelo decides to study, she makes new female and male friends, changes her ideas about sexual relations, and, as far as possible, transforms her personal environment in each decision and opportunity she takes. Even if we, as individuals or as groups, cannot control the consequences of some of our actions, we can anticipate them, or at least choose the situations whose results will be most favorable to our interests. This is the basis for transformational social actions. Nevertheless, Chelo's objective is not to transgress but to gain personal relationships that are more gratifying, free, and egalitarian, to broaden her horizons, and raise her expectations. The results of this transformative process should make it possible for others to have free choices, so that the experience of new levels of freedom increasingly favors norms that regulate aggressive behavior against people's freedom and dignity, such as rape. The consequences of her objectives are a result of adequate decisions. To what degree can we accept uncertainty, necessary for change, without risking our control over our actions? The changes in what is the "possible," the "livable," are not based on a systematic transgression of all norms, but on an implicit or explicit agreement among the people who are affected by it on a daily basis. In practice, it is dialogue with others, reflection, and common sense that will guide Chelo till the point at which she can advance toward prospects as yet unimaginable.

We agree that established gender norms play a legitimizing function in life choices, traditionally heterosexual, as well as that they need to be transformed. If the relations between masculine and feminine gender roles seem problematic, one possible solution is to detect their boundaries and make them permeable to each other, deconstruct the edifice of normative/normalizer, showing its artificiality, and develop a normative aspiration that is more free and open than has ever been known by humankind. On the other hand, the establishment of certain categories has excluded many groups of people, whose behavior questions the natural character of this binary worldview that forgets the nuances and plurality of what is human. Thus, this deconstruction process would lead to the transformation of gender relations proposed by Butler, based on a questioning of the constrictions of sexual differences, which would stop them from being seen as natural, and on the creation of new spaces that reject a binary distribution of gender.

The problem lies in whether the acceptance of plurality—the transformation of this binary reductionism and the assumption of freedom—involves a nonattachment from an identity and nonconformity against the norms of such an attachment. Butler herself provides an answer when she talks about the dual avenues to follow with respect to gender in the politics of human rights: to refer to a language that calls attention to the urgency of this question and, at the same time, to submit the categories that constitute it to a critique that questions its limits, its foundational framework, and the possibilities of its opening.

A quick evaluation of the accomplishments of the women's movement illustrates how the fight for normative and legislative progress has supposedly made appreciable advances in terms of labor, sexual freedom, and an unprecedented transformation in gender relations. The "other women" must fight every day so these rights that have been won can become real in their daily lives. Therefore, we cannot stop at questioning only gender norms and identities in an absolute sense, but ultimately also those rights that are still not reflected in the lives of many women. We suspect that the solution will come from the possibility of introducing an opening to the other and the use of reflection as independent variables in our guiding concepts.

I enthusiastically share Judith's explicit separation from a relativist reductionism that would consider even human rights an unnecessary norm or one that should not be universal. I agree with the need to break from the constraints of gender norms, and also that the current formulation of human rights must be revised to eliminate the constrictions of its predominantly masculine and Western orientation, which has silenced other voices that are essential for the creation of truly universal human rights.

The dialogic perspective that I set out attempts to show how it is possible, through constant reflection, to elaborate norms that incorporate tools to differentiate undesirable behavior such as rape. I already mentioned in my first text in this book that some movements of "other women" are preparing declarations of rights in concrete spheres; I also incorporated some of the reflections of Gypsy women's associations on what reformulations of human rights would best serve their being heard and not ignored. The dynamic by which these proposals and reflections can be taken into account is what I call the equality of differences,

whose objectives with regard to gender categories are: (1) to foster a new panorama of coexistence between different identities
that is not centered on ignorance of the other, and (2) to clarify
the mechanisms for implementing a process for the reformulation of gender roles.

Judith and I defend the need for questioning the limits of the
categories of gender and identity in general, and we are also seeking ways of profoundly taking on this opening, although we approach it from different directions. From a deconstructionist perspective, you can emphasize an indeterminate factor in the
definition of identity norms, assuming ignorance in contact with
the different. I prefer to reinforce the establishment of mechanisms for the redefinition (not a blurring) of these categories,
trusting in the possibility of an understanding and recognition of
that which is different, such that the image that is collabora-
tively constructed is grounded in an equally collaborative model,
with both ends sharing in the possibility of an opening toward
the middle and creating spaces in which dialogue and transformation is possible without having to renounce one's own category of identity.

So, I would like to qualify that sustainability and harmony
between different options of identity is guaranteed by the acceptance of mutual ignorance and estrangement. By this view, respect for the other person is possible only by maintaining her
foreign character. I believe, on the other hand, that in the need to
redefine the norms that constitute identities, it is precisely the
proximity and consideration of the foreign that implies a truly
transformative opening. As I said in the earlier text, I understand
this reflexive process in the context of a "second modernity," a
reflexive modernity, which incorporates a factor of indetermina-
tion and constant reformulation while emphasizing the value of
rationality.

On this point I bring to mind an instance of radical overstep-
ping of the limits between the categories of masculine and feminine that occurred precisely in the modern era: In the Paris of the
1930s and '40s, Lucy Schwob, aka Claude Cahun, shaped her identity in this way, with masculine and feminine elements that were
profoundly transgressive in their combination, even by today's
standards; hers was a blunt expression of sexual ambivalence and
of questioning the limits of identity. As I state in my first text,
modernity has developed as it dissolved through questioning. In

the second modernity, reflection adopts new dimensions, with the centrality of the intersubjective and the possibility for human agency to interact with the social systems. This implies a social responsibility in structural changes, as well as the necessity for the systems to consider the existence of human rights. Reflection generates social transformation when it is shared collectively and intersubjectively.

In this way, consensus can replace ignorance, and recognition can replace estrangement. These replacements do not have to betray or negate difference. It is possible to recognize the other through dialogue.

The relationship outlined above between Laia and Chelo is one of the many examples that illustrate the transformation of intragender relations and the resistance to categories falsely imposed as natural ones. For women in modern democracies, the right to vote, the right to an education, and the right to choose our relationships are assumed. What remains is for these rights to become prevalent in democratic systems. Among the demands articulated in many of the "other women's" movements are those that take the prevailing feminism a step further: These demands raise the possibility of being a feminist and a coquette, a "mother" and independent, to not have an academic education and to demand one, to not occupy a position of "power" yet dare to talk in public academic spaces, to go out in a miniskirt and denounce those who legitimize rape. The women who make these demands engage in intragender relationships on the basis of the capacity to establish an egalitarian dialogue, and their choices, made through consensus, liberate us and help us keep going in the face of all that labels us and makes us give up.

I share with Judith a recognition of the urgent need for the full plurality of voices in order to attain real social transformation in gender relations and on the path toward nonviolence. Is there only one way of living the feminine experience? Everyday reality presents us with experiences of being a woman or a man that differ from "normality." So too for the "other women," who are subjected to prejudice even within feminism. Many of their voices are calling for the definition of new forms of gender, to overcome normativity and categorization that can limit our life's project. We must break with these limits, so that our identities are not constrained and we do not feel violated. Judith points out correctly that drag represents the questioning of the limits between the feminine and the masculine, which at times awakens vehement reactions in its conflict with the established norm. As an assurance of respect for the development of these new genders from the dialogic feminist perspective, we defend a redefinition of identities that can guarantee the recognition and freedom of those "others," male and female, who are ignored or as of yet not possible. In order for these new forms of gender to be included, which is proposed by dialogic feminism, it is necessary to have a common framework and principles that are jointly agreed upon, so that the space we share does not drift toward indifference between people and groups. To overcome current limits to inclusiveness, it is necessary to *understand* these "other" strangers or "unknowns," and also *learn* from them to radicalize ethical and social transformation.

In September 1999 I attended, along with a group of nonacademic women, a meeting of women's associations from Catalonia. In one of the debates, a participant in the movement of "other women" spoke up to publicly reflect on the fact that many women like herself felt excluded from the feminist discourses and demands. The response she received from the speaker was: "We are all housewives. This is the nucleus of oppression." In this way, the speaker closed the subject in a corporate manner, instead of seriously considering the request of the plaintiff, which is widespread among a large number of women who are also claiming feminism for themselves. By denying the issue specific to the "other women," the speaker rejected taking on the issue of the alienation of the majority of women from debates that only some of us have the power to generate. The danger of the speaker's response is its demagogic character. It is important to know which constraints are common to *all of us,* in order to avoid relativisms, as Judith also warns us. In this way we will create possibilities for a social transformation that requires a universal and open debate.

To assure the radical recognition of this plurality of voices also requires shared spaces that are based on an exchange and understanding between different communities. Therefore, the people and groups with distinct life projects must agree on certain basic principles. Far from constraining our experiences and coercing our decisions, this common, consensual framework can expand our freedom of action. The FACEPA women's group that I used as an example in the first chapter defends and works under this criterion. This federation of associations constitutes a forum in which women of different ages and cultural backgrounds participate. All of them nevertheless share the same desire: through dialogue, to transform gender relations that affect them and open up possibilities that they can't yet imagine.

The equality of differences is characterized by horizontal relations among women of diverse educational levels and cultures and different genders, oriented toward learning and mutual respect that break with many of the barriers and situations of oppression. Mutual knowledge that derived from this dialogue deepens social transformations in gender inequalities and radicalizes freedom for all of us to be who we want to be. This implies taking hold of the reins in the transformation of our identities and life projects.

The recognition of the possibility of different identities through interactions, and the opening to identities yet to come, strengthens the collective action of movements based on gender identity and endows it with transformative meaning. What I have learned and am learning through my participation with the groups of "other women" is transforming me. It is this process of attentive and serene listening and the experience of including diversity and exchanging ideas and opinions on the basis of it that can bring us to a joint redefinition of identities and expand our conceptions of the other.

However, in this dialogue we need certain prior conditions that ensure that this recognition does not hinder its sustainability and coexistence. Thus we are thankful for the dialogic turn that societies are taking, just as in the case of dialogic feminism. By becoming dialogic, societies are on the way to overcoming the hegemonic barriers of traditional modernity, whose exclusionary inertias seek to eschew the validity of dialogic arguments. Systemic barriers could also pose opposition, rejecting the submission to reflection and dialogue of certain structural elements of societies. The dialogic turn is not based on power claims, which is the defining aspect of identity for Foucault, but is grounded in validity claims that are brought into play in situations of negotiation, which are increasingly more numerous. The energy that gives life to these dialogic situations is oriented toward the power of arguments and not arguments of power. This reflexive and dialogic framework provides a constant redefinition of the categories of the second modernity, as defined by authors like Ulrich Beck. In my prior works, I have insisted on surmounting the inertial tendencies of traditional modernity, and I consider the reflections that Judith makes about the "radically democratic" redefinition of categories to be very close to my contributions and in accordance with the dialogic turn.

To progress in the dialogic perspective, there needs to be egalitarian respect (not homogenization) for the different life options of people, as individuals and as collectives. On occasion our points of view will not coincide, but we have previously agreed on what differences are sustainable, in the sense that our life's project does not oppress or exclude the other.

We must keep in mind that plurality is not possible if it is based on an imposition. In this case, the possibilities of alternative identities would not truly be optional and inclusive. Neither is real plurality possible with indifference. This would occur if we considered that what characterizes us as women is the *cause* and not the *consequence* of the oppression. Indifference is concerned with either the abolition of "the feminine" (which would not be "different") or a lack of committment to difference. The confluence of both has been paralyzing for women's movements, as is evident when some women occupy social spaces that up until now have been denied to the feminine and yield their own identity without a critique of this renunciation. In the equality of differences, we witness a model whose strength lies in flexibility, the capacity for the inclusion of the plural, and the assumption of a social subject capable of acting consciously in an individual life and in the social arena.

In our work of dialogue, opening to the other, and transformation, we do not seek to dissolve the multiple and very diverse elements that make up people's different identities, because not defining them would not bring about nonviolence or end situations of oppression. The cause of our oppression is not identities, but the context in which they exist. In order to end oppression, we have to orient our actions toward the eradication of conditions that situate us in unequal positions.

Obviously, the needs of different people and collectives may vary, but all of them are governed by the will to develop in complete freedom and be recognized. This recognition is fed by certain rules that require respect for everybody and by making possible, as Judith Butler asserts, the complexity of genders. The dynamic that must take place with regard to this, which, in fact,

diverse social movements are both demanding and attaining, is a
continuous participation in the collective reformulation of
human rights: principles agreed upon that guarantee freedom.
Many women in Gypsy women's movements assert that they do
not want to stop being women or Gypsy while at the same time
claiming the right to transform all the situations and groups that
infringe upon their capacity for decision making and self-
expression.

Therefore, this philosophy of freedom needs a gauge, a norm, a
measure, but one that is in accord with all the voices involved in
the process of dialogue and is as open as possible to the incorporation of new expressions of self-determination. The "livable
life" would be no more than a project of constant redefinition,
except in its capacity as an agreed-upon project and as the result
of decision making oriented toward the sustainability of respect
for the right to the equality of differences.

⌘

Women can transform the norms and ideals of gender through
processes of reflection generated in interactions with other
women. Transformative actions must arise from defining the
possibilities and future avenues for women, rethinking one's
own life conditions (social and personal) and those of others, and
proposing individual and collective changes. In this process,
identities are platforms from which action and understanding are
possible. An identity binds a group of people who recognize
themselves on that basis and who collaborate for specific common ends related to their own survival and, oftentimes, that of
other groups. In adopting an identity, shared aspirations become
amplified to create concrete realizations. Thus, human agency
and the social subject arise from interaction with other people
from groups and not so much through individual processes. So,
that is why there is a need to invoke the right to identities in
order to overcome exclusion based on gender. To move beyond
looking to a manipulating hand to categorize identities, we as
people and collectives must assume the capacity of reformulating these particularities.

It is true that gender identity implies a strong generalization,
which ignores certain individual or idiosyncratic ways of life,
and that it is easy for it to be lived as a failure, since it supposes

an ideal, a model, which is impossible to fully attain. But, the individualities within social groups notwithstanding, the most disadvantaged groups will always build their social claims on the basis of being bound together by identity traits (for example, battered women). Thus, putting into practice the implications of the discussion regarding the need to transgress the limits of gender norms that make up the different identities is not as useful among groups of women from highly oppressed social contexts as it is for social groups that are governed by more open democratic premises. A majority of humanity would not have the opportunity of practicing an extreme relativization of the gender norms, that is, a sexual indifference or nondifferentiation.

Once feminism understood the possibility and necessity for reformulating gender categories, it rejected certain traits that constituted an identity, for example the feminine, believing that these traits were responsible for women's exclusion. The construction of the feminine has incorporated certain values associated with certain feelings, such as sensuality, which are not regarded as instruments for social competitiveness in the current state of things, and thus, have simply been rejected. On the other hand, certain manifestations of masculine oppression against women have not been radically questioned. On the contrary, they have been perpetuated, by both men and women, as optimal expressions of positions of power, instead of being submitted to deeper reflection to eliminate this oppression. Thus some women have proclaimed the need to take on certain negative masculine roles instead of questioning their viability in a more egalitarian future.

The "other women" live in serious conditions of inequality. When the feminist movement emerged, society in general and progressive movements in particular questioned the identity of women on which our women's movements were based. The pretext for the questioning was that all of us—men and women—are people. The feminist movement replied that the way toward the recognition of everybody's rights depends, fundamentally, on the identification of the rights that women have. It was the only way in which the inequalities that women suffer were made evident, and it was only through working for the expression of women's voices and the recognition of their rights that we moved toward equality. Similarly, nowadays, new movements are claiming their identity, as is that of "other women"; it is the only way to make their inequality visible even within the women's movements, and therefore, the only way to fight against that inequality.

On the one hand, gender identities designated by *norms* define our sexual behaviors and manifestations. On the other hand, the expression of gender categories, including sexual behavior, affects the building of these identities, according to the redefinition of the norms that mark them. This dual conception of society seems important to me, in that the subject's actions can affect the world of structures. However, I would like to comment on some important aspects about the terms in which these exchanges are developed. A dual society defined by its structures is conceived according to the social demands that make human agency possible (based on social movements, citizen participation, etc.). However, it is more difficult for me to understand the capacity for social transgression in an individual sexual behavior. Thus, a butch/femme relationship would be transformative only if it has social repercussions. If not, these behaviors or concrete expressions of identity would become a kind of ritual aimed, on certain occasions, at dismantling the barriers within gender through a combination of ceremony and political project. However, the political project of the "other women" is in their public claim as nonacademic women, emphasizing the specificity of their gender and their social condition, according to which they demand recognition as individuals and a collective; they are committed to the struggle for the transformation of the structures and conditions that perpetuate the unequal situations they face.

For the "other women," this social dimension is fundamental to making possible real alternatives to concrete situations. How can we eliminate gender violence if we do not identify those who define the power that feeds it, and thus the social mechanisms that would relieve it? This would be possible by using consensus, rationality, dialogue, and validity arguments to redefine the limits of the categories that order the ideals of gender.

Regarding the understanding of the heterosexual as a constitutive element of the perception of reality, if hierarchies exist through language, behaviors, etc., and gender identities have the function of "domesticating us" on the deepest level, it is fair to ask by what authority this is being done and how we can escape from a vicious cycle according to which everything is defined by a heterosexual or dichotomist form of thinking. How can we get enough distance to see clearly the oppression to which women are submitted, as well as the solution to this conflict?

The proposals of the movements of "other women," when they are taken into account, show how, in fact, we may escape certain inertias of the structures: by identifying problems, specifying solutions, and assuming social and public responsibility. When the "other women" make explicit the inequality that they suffer in access to education and in entering the labor market, and they formulate concrete demands about how to solve these issues or about the kind of training they want and demand egalitarian treatment through concrete guidelines, we are witnessing a fight, individually and collectively, to part with established gender categories—"established," that is true, by other previous individual and collective fights that also pushed the limits of gender categories.

The goal is to create spaces of freedom and expression on the basis of equality, especially for the women who suffer an exponential inequality (the "other women") based on their condition as nonacademic or minority-culture or both. In this book, authors with different trajectories have generated an interesting exchange of ideas, and we have tried to contribute elements to the definition of the mechanisms that can guide the future of dialogic feminism and social transformation. Consequently, now we have to complement and enrich what we have said by eliminating any distance between the women our works address and the works themselves. One way may be by multiplying the meeting spaces between women of different ages, cultures, academic levels, etc., as did the Women and Social Transformation conference, from which this book arose. The next step will be to include the perspectives of the "other women" into our work. These women's contributions most successfully contradict an image of feminism devoid of the real problems of women, of *all* women.

References

Aliaga, J. V. 1997. *Bajo vientre. Representaciones de la sexualidad en la cultura y el arte contemporáneos.* "La problemática de los géneros sexuados en el arte contemporáneo. Algunas notas sobre lo *queer,* con permiso de Judith Butler." Valencia: Generalitat Valenciana.

Butler, J. 1990. *Gender Trouble: Feminism and the Subversion of Identity.* New York: Routledge.

Butler, J. 1993. *Bodies that Matter: On the Discursive Limits of "Sex."* New York: Routledge.

Butler, J. 2000. *Antigone's Claim.* New York: Columbia University Press.

Cooper, D., Faye, J. P., Faye, M. O., Foucault, M., and Zecca, M. 1977. Dialogue sur l'enfermement et la répression psychiatrique. *Change,* 32–33, pp. 76–110. Paris: Collectif Change.

Derrida, J. 1989. *De la Gramatología.* Madrid: Siglo XXI (original 1967).

Flecha, R. 2000. *Sharing Words: Theory and Practice of Dialogic Learning.* Lanham, Md: Rowman & Littlefield Publishers.

Foucault, M. 1988. *Nietzsche, la genealogía y la historia.* Valencia: Pretextos (original 1968).

CHAPTER 6

Gender and Social Transformation: A Dialogue[1]

Preliminary Remarks

LÍDIA PUIGVERT: I would like to start just with a brief and concrete explanation, because the aim of this panel is to open the debate to all of us. Basically, the first thing I wanted to say is that when Judith sent me her papers, which we then published as a book, I saw in them reflections and contributions that prompted me to initiate several conversations. I hope that Judith and I continue to bring those debates to subsequent encounters, or subsequent intellectual works such as the one we're initiating here. But due to the limited time we have—which includes time we should leave for debate with everyone here—I will limit myself to explaining basically three points that I consider to be focal to this conference and the debates we have had during this day and a half. I will zero in on these three themes also for the plurality of voices of the women who are represented here. The three points I will speak about are the following:

Firstly, one of the things that I liked most about the work that Judith sent me is her proposal for an international dialogue—"to open an international dialogue," using her exact words, to discuss these issues that concern us all: feminist theory and the task of social transformation, the politics of inclusion, radical democracy, and the inclusion of social movements. This is clearly something that encouraged me, it inspired me, and I sincerely liked that about her work. There are moments, for Judith as much as for me, as well as for Elisabeth, when we see that dialogue will have a primordial and key role in initiating the turning point of what will be the feminist theory of the twenty-first century. I believe that the three of us agree about this. In fact, in her second work, Judith also discusses that a feminist position must also include social transformation, and therefore I am convinced that we have the common assumption that dialogue implies transformation. I would like to focus on this for a moment.

Despite having read Judith's previous works, from the moment we started this dialogue over papers, and especially since she has been here, I have also been transformed, I mean, I have also experienced here what she proposes about self-transformation through dialogue, I have experienced it through reflection about her contributions. In other words, we generate social transformation from the dialogue that we are initiating here. And this process of transformation I think is worth mentioning, because in the same way I am transformed through the dialogues and reflections with Judith, I have also been transformed by women like Emilia, the Gypsy woman who was here yesterday. In fact I have been undergoing transformation from the contributions and dialogues that I have had with these "other women" for a long time. I think it is important to show that with contributions like that of Emilia's yesterday, I keep learning many things that tell me that there is a path on which we can all coincide and meet.

The second point I wanted to make I suppose both Judith and Elisabeth are in agreement with me about, but I also ask them to correct me if I am wrong. The point is that the feminism of the twenty-first century should include the voices of all women, the plurality of all their voices, in the forums that discuss women's issues. In my opinion, the future forums we plan or those that already exist should include the voices of women with academic degrees as well as the voices of other women, like the ones who spoke on the panel earlier today. I think this is something important, and I would like to propose here that we start from this point.

I consider—just like other social scientists, like Habermas or Chomsky—that all women have the capacity for dialogue and transformation. We should not exclude anyone from this dialogue, not one single woman, not Emilia or Fatima or any of the women who have been here. We should initiate it all together. They have made it clear that they know what they want and how they want it, that they have this capacity for dialogue and transformation. In fact, I don't think that any of us remain unperturbed, for example, by the reflections they made earlier on the panel or the reflections Emilia made yesterday from her position as a Gypsy woman. I think we should consider their contributions as important to initiate the feminism of the twenty-first century.

Thirdly, I would like to propose another debate, although this may not be the moment to get into it. In fact, I do not aim to arrive at a consensus, but just to initiate it and maybe to continue this debate in future encounters. We have been talking a lot about dialogue in the last day and a half, but there is still an issue that remains inconclusive: how we construct this dialogue among everyone. During the conference, there have been some reflections here along these lines, but I want to set out my position. I think that social relationships can be organized in various ways, either more connected to power claims or more connected to validity claims. Habermas also takes this position. To briefly explain my stance with regard to this in relation to dialogue, I will use two examples. The first example is related to rape and the second example is related to research on social sciences and gender studies.

When we talk about having sexual relations based on validity claims, this means that everyone who will have these sexual relations agrees, they are in agreement about having these relations, they agree on doing it. On the contrary, a relationship based on power claims would imply that even though a person says "no," the relationship is imposed on this person. Rape is a relation based on power claims, and therefore I oppose them.

The second example is related to how we produce knowledge in social sciences and specifically in gender studies. To explain my position here, I will refer to one of the comments that was made from the audience this morning in which the person speaking explained how we are conducting research in one of our studies, the Workaló project, an RTD research project coordinated by us, from CREA, and funded by the Fifth Framework Program of the European Union. Research can be conducted in very different ways. In traditional modernity, research in social sciences used to investigate, for example, Gypsy women, without taking them into account, like mere objects to be "studied." Like Emilia said yesterday, and other women this morning, researchers ask questions and often get what they are interested in, but they interpret other people's lives through their own lenses and then they leave. By contrast, what happens in *our* research is that Gypsy women directly participate in the project, and from the beginning to the end, on the lines of dialogic feminism. This means that participants are involved with us in each phase: the research design, the objectives, the data analysis, and the conclusions, like Ana said this morning, from beginning to end. The first type of research I mentioned would be a typical project based on academic hierarchies, in which one investigates and interprets what others think. *Our* research is based on validity claims, which means that the thoughts of all the women are included, regardless of their academic background.

I guess that in these three points I have included the main reflections that came to my mind while engaging in dialogue with Judith, which I hope will set out some interesting issues for the debate.

⊗⊗⊗

JUDITH BUTLER: First of all, I want to thank everyone who was responsible for inviting me here. This has been, for me, a quite singular experience and I will leave here not the exact same person I was when I came. I think this transformation will take place in many ways. Three days ago I probably would have simply said: "No entiendo español," and today I say: "Entiendo poco español." But I think "entiendo" is the most important verb for me right now: What do I understand, what do I not understand? You have shown me some of the limits of my understanding, and for that I am grateful. I think it would be a terrible thing if I knew myself so well that I did not stand the chance of being changed. So, I thank you for this. I have been reflecting on many of the statements that people have made. I've been very moved, extremely moved by the voices that I've heard. This morning, when we heard about literacy, I saw and heard what it means for some women to learn to read. It takes me back to the basic, perhaps the most fundamental, tenet of feminism, which has to do with a sense of empowerment. So, from "no puedo leer" to "puedo leer," this is an enormous social transformation. Sometimes we think, oh, social transformation must have some global cataclysmic form. But, "puedo leer"—that is a revolution. I mean, I think it can be a revolution. So, I wanted to speak just about a few things that have occurred to me in relation to

Elisabeth's paper, which I found very interesting, and Lídia's challenges in her thinking, which I think are enormously far-reaching and significant.

But let me start just by suggesting that for some of my students, especially older women, who have been working their whole lives and have returned to the university—by the way, they're always my best students, because they know why they are there—it is one thing to say, "I am a university woman." It is another thing to say, "I go to the university." If one says, "I go to the university," that does not mean that all I am is a university woman, because I may also work, I may also have a family, I may also care for other people who are not my family. The "I," who attends the university, seems to me to be a very complex thing, and when we take classes, go to the university, study, learn, and make this our identity—"I am a university woman"—it may be that we erase parts of our lives which are very important and, in fact, parts of our lives that connect us with other women. So, certainly, I am Judith Butler. I am an academic. I cannot lie. You could say, "I am an academic woman," and I will even say that. But, as you may know, to be a woman is for me . . . it is hard. It is difficult. I say it, I have solidarity, but I have to tell you, I am on an edge. I'm on a margin. But I will say it, for you, for us, in public, for the newspaper, but I have to tell you, it is difficult for me. Not because I hate being a woman, but because, for me, there are ideas of what a woman is that I cannot recognize myself in. So, for instance, we have heard from "otras mujeres" here, in this wonderful conference, but I have heard no one say, "I am a lesbian." Why not? Why is that not speakable? Or is that speakable? Can it be said? Is that included under the notion of "other women"? I have not heard from the prostitutes, whose work is not considered decent work. I mean, most of us are decent, most of us are proper, even though we may be working class and may be having lots of problems. But what about the women who work in areas where there is shame, where there is public ostracism or marginalization? I have not heard from the marginalized sexual communities. There may be transvestites who would be much happier than I to say "I am a woman." It might be much easier for them. Do we want to think about this when we think about "mujeres"? Who says I am a woman? Who can say it? Who says it easily? Who says it with difficulty? When do we allow people to say it? Who do we include in our notion of "mujeres"? These seem to me to be important questions, so maybe, as this is a movement, this dialogue between academic and nonacademic women should expand, and we should maybe think about the other "other." That is, the other women who are not even part of the "other women." I think that would be interesting and important to do. If one were not to say, "I am a university woman" . . . well, one must say it to mark one's place, one's privilege, one's power. On the other hand, if we begin to tell a life story—if some of you from the audience began to tell life stories, and some of you on this panel also began to tell life stories—it seems to me that there is always a question of whether we have gone to university or not, where we work, what kind of families we have, what our life situations are. And then the idea "I am a nonacademic woman," "I am an academic woman," it seems to me that these categories of identity become more complex when we start to tell stories. It turns out that some of us come to the university from poverty, some of us maybe go to the university to study or to teach but go back to marriages where there is violence, some of us have gone to the university but had to quit in order to work. There are stories. It seems to me that the story, the narrative, may give a richer sense of who we are and what our commonalities are than the simple assertion of identity.

I would like to say briefly something about the question of power and agency. I think that, in Spanish, "puedo" (I can) and "poder" (power) are connected. It seems to me that when Lídia says that every woman has the capacity to think and to act, we must accept this as true. But if we say that this capacity has nothing to do with power, then I think we miss a very important political point. Because I would add to this claim that there must be conditions which permit the exercise of thinking, of acting, in order for that thinking and acting to become realized, for it to become real. Otherwise, it is simply an abstraction. To say that I can think, that I can act, that I can read, that I can participate in social transformation, is not just a question of my having the personal strength and capacity to do that. There must be institutions that support me. There must be conditions of power which enable me. So that this very university, by opening up its room to "las otras mujeres," and giving its "mesa redonda" to women who are nonacademics to speak, this is what I would call a good use of power. It is power in the sense of what enables us, and it is even a productive use of power. It would be a mistake for feminists to think that power is only violence, or that power is only domination. As academic women, we do have the power to open up this institution, to give these microphones away, to invite people in who do not regularly come to the university, and to hand over the conversation. Even to yield power is a use of power. We should not be afraid of power. Power does not belong solely to men. It is not bad, necessarily. It can be good and it can be used, and we must not be afraid to use it. I think many women would like to think of women's studies or women's spaces as free from power, that we have nothing to do with power, that power is what men have. That is not true. We must avow the way we use power in order to use it well. There is an obligation for women in privileged positions to use power well. So I would dispute the notion that power equals violence, or that power equals domination. If we allow those equations to stand, then we lose the capacity to use power well. It seems to me that when we talk about whether women can act or whether they have agency, we are always asking whether the social conditions under which they live permit a certain kind of agency or do not permit it. It is why our personal transformation is dependent on social transformation. So, whatever my individual capacity is, it makes no difference unless I am able to live in a world which allows me to realize it.

I think that Elisabeth, in her paper, was very honest when she said that when she first began her research, she assumed that immigrant wives were in positions of powerlessness, that their marriages were contracts probably without love, and that the women were probably in these marriages without any sense of freedom or agency. But what she found, as she became closer to the real situations of these women, was that there was some agency, there was some capacity to negotiate their situations. They also had aims—they were trying to accomplish things. They were trying to leave misery. They were trying to realize ideals. They were trying to open up a future not only for themselves but for their families. So they were not all pure victims in this situation. Elisabeth was very careful, but at least she said some of them were not. That situation strikes me as a way we might approach the question of how we can become capable of social transformation. The women about whom she writes and with whom she works are constrained. They are economically disenfranchised. They are compelled to marry in order to leave their misery or achieve their economic and life goals. And yet, we might say they are constrained but they are not purely victimized, that their agency emerges precisely from this situation of constraint, and that they live both at once. This is important because we might see here that power—the power of the economy, the power of patriarchy, of geopolitical realities, all of which constrains them—also allows marriage to a German man to be an economic option. They are constrained but their fates haven't been determined, that is to say, they still have some freedom, they still have some capacity to negotiate, to strategize, to think about what they want and how best to get it. So, there again, I would say that what we understand as their capacity to act and to think is connected intrinsically to the conditions of power within which they live. But power does not negate freedom, nor does freedom fully overcome power. They work together.

Finally, I do not want to have an academic discussion about the big men who stand behind us, Habermas and Foucault. It does not matter. I do not belong to Foucault and I hope Lídia does not belong to Habermas. I don't think we should be defending our men. Foucault is rich for me, but I use him. He cannot think in terms of sexual violation. I would never look to Foucault for a theory of sexual violation. You are absolutely right. On the other hand, if we think about how many countries there are which imprison homosexuals for being psychiatrically pathological, or we think about how often homosexuality is understood as a social pathology which is subject to imprisonment, psychiatric internment, or state violence—and this works very differently for men and women, but it works against both—then, certainly, I would say one must look to Foucault. But that is all I care about. And I guess I would urge you, as you continue to democratize your movement, to think about the prostitutes who work in this area at night, to bring them in. They have much to say. I am sure there are unionization efforts here—there are internationally. I would think about gender politics more broadly. What kinds of street violence are the transvestites in Barcelona subject to, have we thought about that? Do the lesbian and gay students in this university, or those who work outside, do they have a voice within feminism? Is that perhaps another voice that needs to be heard? That's all.

ELISABETH BECK-GERNSHEIM: I would like to talk about two points, which obviously came up in the first panel this morning. First of all, who are the "other women"? And the definition that came up from CREA was that they are women without higher education. This kind of dichotomy, women with or without higher education, does this mean that we are organizing the world and seeing the world according to a binary code, as we say in theory? That is a dichotomy, like either "men" or "women." So you either have higher education or you are outside of it. We do know that there are problems with this way of seeing the world. For instance, there are women who are scrubbing floors in order to earn the money to be able to get a university degree, so where do they fit in? And I just want to make clear that the dichotomy doesn't fit for the women I was talking about yesterday either—for migrant women. Many migrant women have degrees from home—they were teachers, nurses, etc., but when they go abroad and they do domestic work, they are badly paid, and they have bad working conditions, they have no social security. So in one sense they are privileged, and in another sense they are very much discriminated against. So where does this leave us, and where does this leave them? To me it means that the dichotomy does not hold. And we have to find new categories and new terms that represent the complexity of women's lives, just as Judith said before. There is a whole story and we cannot put it into one label because that is too simplistic.

Again, coming to the label "other women," my second point is, who brought up this term? I heard that it obviously comes from the group itself, but I have to confess that when I heard this label before, I really did have difficulties with it because a parallel discussion came to my mind: the ongoing discussion in the U.S. on race. There is a discourse on race in which there are categories like black, white, Hispanic, Indian, which presupposes that you are either one or the other. And I tell you, there are lots of people who just do not fit into either one category or the other because they come from different backgrounds, from different parents so to speak. So where does it leave them? On official forms they had to subscribe to a term like "other" because they did not fit the official categories. Then, they went up and said, "We are not 'other,' we are people, this is nonhuman and we don't want to be called 'others,'" and now they dropped this category from some official forms. So this is why I have difficulties with this label of "other women." But when it comes up from themselves, it is different.

Then, my third point is about dialogic feminism. As we know, it means that we listen to other voices, other experiences. And in one sense I do represent another voice, and another experience, the experience from another country, from Germany. And I would like to give you my experience of feminism in Germany today. What I hear from Lídia and what I hear from you are optimistic voices, a feminism that is alive, and very much so. I have to say that the situation in Germany is different. And this will add a question for you, Judith: How is it in the States? In Germany, nowadays, I would not say the feminist movement is dead, because some of my best friends would kill me for that, but it is definitely not a very lively and active social movement anymore. Especially not for the younger women. And I would even dare to say that it has become a dirty word to them. They do not want to be called feminist. They say, "Feminist . . . that was my mother's generation. Oh my god, they always talked about being victims and being oppressed, I'm not a feminist." And this goes for my students too—they are definitely not attracted to anything called feminism. Some years ago, I used to give courses on feminist topics, and I do not do this anymore because I know that very few people will attend. I mean, men would never attend and very few women would attend. So I do it differently. I give courses on broader subjects, like the labor market or family, and then, of course, there are sessions on women and family, or on women in the labor market or whatever. But, it is not very appreciated, I have to tell you. They may attend because they have to, for curricular requirements, but there is no light in their eyes when we discuss these topics. I then ask myself why my students are not interested anymore. As I said before, feminism to them is the image of being a victim, being oppressed, and their experience is different. They are now in the educational system. In the educational system there is real equality, there is even a slightly higher number of women who go to university or have a degree than men. And during their university years, while they are studying, not after they get the degree, there is no discrimination, and they think, "Well, what is all this talk about? Where is this discrimination?" and say, "Look, stop talking about discrimination, wake up, it's the twenty-first century." Then, of course, I can say, "Grow up, little girls, just wait and see when you get to the labor market, just wait and see when your boyfriend becomes a husband, or if you become a single mother and need to be in the labor market. Then, what will happen to you? Your situation will be different." But this sounds awful. It sounds like I'm being my own grandmother. So, I do not dare to say this. That is my difficulty. How can I do dialogic feminism with them? Who are the important ones? They are the young generation, but they do not want to go into this kind of discourse. That is my question.

Reactions from Authors

PUIGVERT: Just to remark on something I said in my introduction: It seems to me that the three of us agree that the feminism of the twenty-first century must include many more voices than those included up until now. And in that sense, I am very much in agreement with everything Judith said, that although this forum included for the first time women who have been invisible in feminism and nonexistent in an academic setting like this university, there are still women missing. And my hope is that in the following forum they will be present. For example, lesbian women, who have not manifested publicly in this forum as lesbians—or, following what Elisabeth said, more of a presence of immigrant women like Fatima, the Arab woman who participated in the panel yesterday, or those who took part from the floor. Therefore, I am in agreement with both of my colleagues that it is important that we build the feminism of the twenty-first century with the plurality of voices that represent all the women of today.

❧❧❧

BUTLER: I would add a comment, in response to Elisabeth's question about how to appeal to these young women who want to have nothing to do with feminism. One of the exciting aspects of this meeting has been the focus on transformation, which is active and empowering. Certainly, we have heard about many situations in which there is suffering and disenfranchisement, especially as we hear about women who work. One woman here told

us she works eleven hours a day—I mean, this is unbelievable—
and that she also comes to the conference, and she reads, and
that she is somehow an anarchist, and I bet she does meet with
other anarchists. So, who knows how she sleeps. But the point is
that to move the discourse of feminism from victimization to
transformation is crucial. I think this is why this is not a depress-
ing meeting. This is a hopeful meeting. I think in Germany, as I
have experienced feminism there, the young people feel that
they are being asked to identify with this position of victimization, something that will keep them from having happiness in
life. And that cannot be. Feminism must orient us toward happiness in life if it is to be compelling as a movement.

⧉

BECK-GERNSHEIM: I think that in order to appeal to the younger
students, we would also have to bring up the word "solidarity,"
and that is difficult nowadays in a country like Germany, which
is very much moving toward becoming a new liberal state. Solidarity is out.

Dialogue with the Audience

COMMENT: First of all, I would like to express my satisfaction
about the fact that three authors like yourselves, who are used to
such recognition in the feminist debate on an international level,
are in agreement with each other. In some way you commit to a
feminist theory that is critical and transformative, and for me
this means that whether we women are white, black, lesbian,
heterosexual, prostitutes, or housewives, we have the capacity to
change our situation and to decide the lifestyle we want to lead.
Having said that, I would like to make a comment addressed to
Judith Butler about the fear that you expressed on the first conference day about being considered a postmodern author. You
said, and I quote, "a crazy postmodernist." I don't think there's
any point in your feeling this fear, and I say this because I too
have transformed myself through dialogue, and my vision also
has changed. I have to recognize that at first your insistence on
referring to Foucault in this case shocked me. I do not want to
enter any debate about Foucault and Habermas either, not just

because they are men, but because I do not think it is the objective. But I have to say that from my point of view you do not only use Foucault, which is fine with me, but I think you surpass him by far, in two aspects that for me are fundamental, and which make me distance myself from the Foucauldian theory or from a vision that is more postmodern: Foucault's theory and the concept of power. I think it is very clear that, for Foucault, his theory is an exercise of power; it is a form of power because it objectifies the individual. He converts the individual into an object, he divides it, fragments it, normalizes it, because he has a limited concept of power. For him, power only excludes, discriminates, controls, and represses. I think that you are very far from all of that, and your previous comments made that very clear for me, in the sense that theory is capable of transforming and that power does have a double meaning, the power that excludes and the power that is capable of transforming. Therefore, from a radical feminist theory, we must choose this power that in some way conceptualizes the capacity for a person's agency. But having said this, I think that we would all agree on the fact that power exists, also it must be said that power is unequally distributed. Therefore, in order to transform, we should be concerned about how this power can be distributed, and it must be recognized that, for example, having an academic degree gives you a different kind of power in society. It is not the same to be black or black with studies, white and illiterate, white with an academic degree, lesbian with or without having attended college. I think that this also needs to be expressed, and that captures most of our concerns about the conditions under which power is distributed. Then, why fight against this theme, against this focus? Having said this, and wrapping up, I think that the category "other women" has the capacity to include many women, not just the nonacademic women. I think we have to recognize the significance of this forum, which is better attended, in numbers, than most conferences because it has included a sector that had been totally excluded from them. But this does not mean that the road ends here. I agree with you that we have to continue to work so that this movement becomes more inclusive of all of the sectors that you mentioned. For me, this is the advantage of the "other women," to include the women who have no voice.

BUTLER: Just briefly . . . It is not important, but I think Foucault understood power to be double, not just negative, but also to be productive. I would only say that. I appreciate your comments, and I think I should just let others speak.

∞

COMMENT: First Judith, I would like to make an observation to you about something that concerns me. I am concerned because often I have seen how some of these concepts, of ideas that you have put forth, are trivialized. For example, your concept of "performativity" is trivialized. I think that one cannot speak lightly about changing one's sex three or four times a day. I think it is a bit more serious than that, and often, in our country, it has been trivialized. The suffering that you talk about is not taken sufficiently into account. The reality of how this person lives in her body, her desires, or whatever. Secondly, and changing the topic, before this symposium started, I was also concerned because I assumed the possibility that I was an "other man": on the one hand, because I am gay, and on the other, because I am at a conference about feminism. This felt like a problem for me. How did I solve this problem? On the one hand, I have confidence in the fact that I'm a privileged person because I have the tools to be here and to express what I want to say with a certain precision, because of the luck of having studied. This helped me. On the other hand, I thought about what feminism has contributed throughout history, and we know it has not just been concerned with women. The feminist movement has shown us all how to be more free—gay movements, workers movements, etc. The idea of liberation, transformation, is an idea that can be applied to other social groups. And of course, gay people, we have also brought a lot to feminism. And there is a third thought: I have a friend who is gay, Gypsy, and a gardener in our city, and he is an invisible person. This person exists, but he still does not exist for many people. What is it that will make this person exist?— firstly, forums like this one are created, in which this person would have a place to express himself. So in my opinion, the path is in this direction, toward providing tools to these people so that they can be visible, because if not, they simply do not exist. They are leading a sordid life, a sort of life as if they did not have a right to life. I find this incredibly unjust.

There is still another issue I want to remark about on your talk. You made a comment in the beginning about whether the word "poder" (power) and the word "puedo" (I can) in Spanish had the same root, and you said, "Anyway, they should be the same word." I think that they should be different, because there are two meanings that I think must be distinguished. A fundamental one is the idea of power, the idea of structure, which has more to do with an imposition. Then there's another one that you are not talking about, which is being open to the possibility of dialogue, which has to do with something more than the conjugated form of a verb, I mean, with "I can do that," "I have the possibility of that," "I am open to that," and not as much with a structure that oppresses. I am a bit tired of these discourses that insist too much on structure. For example, I am thinking of a book by Bourdieu, *Masculine Domination*, in which he says that we live in an ether of symbolic violence. But only he, as an author or academic, is able to recognize these elements. Others cannot. I am a bit tired of this. He realizes his contradiction and attempts to say, "Okay, we have to get out of this," but he does not propose any solutions. The solutions are what all of you are saying: the possibility of being open, the possibility of transforming oneself, the focus on dialogue.

∞∞∞

COMMENT: I would like to make a comment on what Elisabeth said about young feminists, the idea that there were no young women wanting to go into feminism. In relation to this, I would like to say a bit about my case. Up until a few years ago I worked dancing in a discotheque, and I thought that all this about feminism was for old-fashioned, bitter women who had nothing better to do, and that I was above all of that. However, I was very mistaken. So, what made me get into feminism? And when I say "into feminism" I am not referring to "Okay, I'm signing up for this," but to experiencing it for real, wanting to fight for it, wanting to keep it alive. Then, what made me get into it was the fact that I saw it was a feminism that really included the voices of all women, where I was included, where my mother was included, my grandmother, my neighbor. It was not a feminism dedicated to a struggle already out of fashion, but one that included all our current concerns. I know that this feeling holds true for me and for many other women like myself. I would like to tell Elisabeth that if this is an issue where she works, I hope dialogic feminism will also spread over there and involve young women, just like here in Spain—there are many young women involved in it. I hope German young women can be encouraged to directly participate in feminism.

※※

COMMENT: I wanted to ask something that is probably a bit unrelated, but I couldn't resist the temptation to ask Judith Butler about it. The question is what is your position in relation to the issue of power, how do you perceive the relationship between sexual desire and the issue of power? Is sexual desire totally constructed by power, or is heterosexuality associated with power, or are there other parameters as well?

※※

BUTLER: I was trying to avoid this topic because I think Lídia and I disagree on that, and it was such a happy party. So, I do not think power is all bad. I have already said that. I do not think power should be identified exclusively with violence, or with domination, although it does take that form, and we must be very mindful of it. Usually, when we think about sexuality and power, we think about sexual violation or sexual domination. But I think there is also an erotic use of power, and I do not believe that the erotic use of power is necessarily heterosexual. I mean, why should heterosexuals be able to enjoy the erotic use of power to the exclusion of everyone else? In any case, I think that anywhere there is vulnerability there is already a question of power, and that one of the things that happens in sexuality—whether it is heterosexual, bisexual, or homosexual—is that there is a negotiation of power. I do not believe we enter into sexual relations as purely deliberative, consenting adults. We do not first think, "how should I desire," and then think "okay, I give permission to my desire." I mean, we find ourselves desiring. And we then decide whether or not to act on it or how to act. But we negotiate something which is already under way. I do not think that any one of us are rational actors, like "oh, I think maybe I will desire so and so today." It just doesn't work that way. But I do think, especially for women, there is always a question of being vulnerable to another, and this is true whether it is a man or a woman. And under what conditions can vulnerability take place? Under what conditions can we assume vulnerability, or assume responsibility for the vulnerability of another? This is power, and sometimes there is something very erotic about negotiating precisely that. What does it mean to yield? What does it mean to take? Is there a way to yield and to take in a way that is not sexual violation? These are erotic questions—they are profoundly erotic questions. They are also questions of power, and I do not believe they are reducible to domination or to violation.

⌘

COMMENT: I would like to make a comment in relation to transsexuality, because there is something that worries me a lot in terms of the question of gender. It is true that transsexuals make a very radical attempt to transform their anatomy in order to subscribe to the gender that they subjectively feel pertains to them. This seems to me to be something that requires a lot of courage. However, it also seems that this attempt does not stop them from being conservative in the sense of a dependency on a certain gender norm. It seems to me, in this case, more courageous to be a homosexual, who does not feel defined by certain social norms that assign him a certain role, a certain identity, a determined way of being, in relation to his anatomy. It could be thus recognized as another way of being, without needing to adapt one's anatomy to a role.

⌘

BUTLER: First, I would say that we are all trying to adapt to anatomy all the time, even if you are born female and you are under the social pressure to become a woman, you spend most of your life trying to adapt to your anatomy, or to adapt your anatomy to the idea of gender. There is a question of working on your body, keeping your weight, doing your hair. My mother used to talk about doing her eyes. I do not know what this means, to do one's eyes, but I gather that that is part of what it is for her to become a woman. She could not go outside without first doing her eyes. So she was all the time trying to adapt her anatomy to a gender norm. And, you know, men too: There is a question of assuming masculinity. We must understand that all of us are engaged in this task in one way or another. So the transsexual is in some ways no different from the ordinary gendered person. It is simply that the transsexual makes it more explicit. This is a radical claim, probably preposterous. I am not sure all gay people accept anatomy. I think many gay people feel like, "yes, this is my anatomy, how can I work with it." There may well be a certain estrangement. One grows up in a culture where the anatomy is supposed to be one way but in fact it is not experienced that way. There is often a renegotiation of meaning of anatomy for gay people, given that we understand our sexual parts to be organized according to a heterosexual function, and they are not. There is already a question: whether some transsexuals do want to return to very conservative notions. A man wants to become a real woman, and wants to idealize a conservative notion of what a woman is; or a woman wants to become a man, wants to be a true man, and has a conservative notion of what a man is. But there are many other ways in which transsexuality is now being played out. Many transsexuals now understand themselves as transforming gender norms. They call themselves transmen or transwomen, suggesting that they are not natural men or women but they are men and women in the process of transformation. Many transsexuals will say that this is a transformation without end. It is a reconception of gender itself as an endless process of transformation. And in this sense they are the inheritors of Simone de Beauvoir's understanding of gender—maybe even the inheritors of feminism to a certain degree in that gender is that which is constantly in transformation. I think that we have seen less conservative, less politically or culturally conservative, forms of transsexuality in recent years.

⚕

COMMENT: I will go back to the general theme of the conference. Those of us who work in fields like adult education, social work, and with social movements I think were able to get many good examples and many good ideas from this conference, and we must take this home and attempt to put it into practice. I would like to add two more things that I circled in my mind during this symposium. One of them is the theme of research. It is true that doing fieldwork in social science research, and particularly in sociology and anthropology, is extremely difficult. But I would not make the distinction between previous and current research—I would rather say that there are good and bad research projects. On the one hand, if researchers conduct bad research, then they interpret, manipulate, and do what they want. If they do it well, the results are clear, positive, committed, etc. On the other hand, I wanted to talk about the dialogic model that I hear you have arrived at. You have arrived at this model through social practice, but not all social practices arrive or lead to the same model and the same theorization. I cannot conceive a theory without social practice. This would be absolutely incorrect, pure ideology. But from social practices that are very similar we arrive at models of feminism that are very different. The proof is that here nobody thinks the same thing, nor do we have the same interpretation of power, authority, dialogue, equality, and it probably takes us to different feminisms. Nevertheless, what is important, I think, is that all of these feminisms hold dialogues. And for me this would be the key to the feminism of the twenty-first century: dialogue. To this effect, Judith Butler used a concept yesterday that seemed extremely important to me; the concept of "cultural translation." It seems to me like a useful concept with a considerable future.

⬦⬦⬦

COMMENT: I hope to express at least what I feel in my heart, what I feel as a working woman and what I feel as a woman in every respect, a feminist, an activist, at all levels. There is something that was not addressed in these symposia, and this is the working woman and her economic situation. There are types of women, like Carolina, who came this morning directly from work in order to be able to come to this conference. And there is a big difference between a woman who has a university career and will probably be able to change her schedule, and Carolina, who had to make an extra effort to attend this conference. She is very tired but she is here. For me, when there is a unification of salaries that does not discriminate against the nonacademic women in favor of the university women, we can move forward together to establish a dialogue about theoretical perspectives for the transformation of society, to make what we are hoping for real: a social revolution.

※

PUIGVERT: To conclude, if there is anything that remains clear to me about this conference, it is that, as it has been said from the audience, we must enter the dialogue. And from this dialogue, we can arrive precisely at what this conference heralds: social transformation for all women.

※

BECK-GERNSHEIM: I will just take up one of the last topics that were brought up. You spoke about research and you said there was good and bad research. I think that this may be a bit too simple because we also have to think about what questions are being asked. I think that feminism is bringing in new questions. I can just give you one example from one field I am working on: reproductive technology. The pioneers from medical sciences and biotechnology say, "Reproductive technology is good, it is good for everybody, it is good for women, it gives them more freedom, it gives them more choice." Then the feminists come and say, "Is this true?" and they bring in new answers. They look into it more closely, they raise their doubts about whether it really holds true, with regard, for instance, to women.

※

BUTLER: I just want to take a minute to thank you again for bringing me here and for allowing me to learn from you. I am afraid I have learned from you much more than you could ever gain from me, and I appreciate what was said about the circumstances under which some people have come to participate in this gathering. I think to work all night and to come to such a gathering must be a very difficult thing. I only hope that, and I certainly can say this for myself, that this meeting will help to give people the energy to sustain the passion that people obviously have here for social transformation. I think, no matter how exhausted we are or how far we need to travel, we need to come together again and again in order to sustain political passion.

And I would also say something that I gathered from this meeting, and this is that many people here who are academics understand their research in terms of a social movement, and many people who are not academics are also here because they ally themselves with a social movement. Maybe this is what needs to come to the fore: how to make a social movement across lines. I think this is a beautiful example, and I am very honored to have been here.

Note

1. This dialogue is the debate that took place in the conference "Women and Social Transformation" among the three keynote speakers: Puigvert, Butler, and Beck-Gernsheim. The authors were asked to first react to the contributions of their colleagues and then open a dialogue. This transcript includes some questions and reactions from the audience, who also contributed to the dialogue.

CHAPTER 7

Feminism for the Twenty-First Century: A Press Conference

Interview with Judith Butler, Lídia Puigvert, Elisabeth Beck-Gernsheim, and Ana Lebrón[1]

What are your first reactions to the conference "Women and Social Transformation"? What would you highlight from this event?

ELISABETH BECK-GERNSHEIM: I would like to stress just one point: It was important that this was a conference where women from different backgrounds came and had a voice. That was a real important thing to do, and I want to thank CREA for that.

JUDITH BUTLER: This was a very rare opportunity for me: to see how women could speak in various ways. Some women spoke about their experience, some spoke about the movements that they are involved in, and others debated intellectual topics, but it seemed to me that they also spoke *to* one another, and they *addressed* one another. They didn't just speak *about* one another. This seems to me very, very important—so that sometimes the academics were in the audience listening to the nonacademic women, and sometimes the nonacademic women were in the audience, but they were also being spoken to. So, I think this structure of address was extremely well done. I have traveled in many countries and gone to many feminist events and I thought this was, perhaps, the most successful event of its kind.

※※※

LÍDIA PUIGVERT: I just want to add to the comments of my colleagues that we also were able to establish a dialogue between academic women and other women, and that we found the way to do it. It seems to me that this is a precedent for the feminism of the twenty-first century. So I hope that there will be more forums like this one, in which the plurality of voices is included, without forgetting the voices of other women who, like Judith said, are in the margins.

※※※

ANA LEBRÓN: To me, it has been very significant that so many important women have been present at the conference. We, the "other women," have been able to say the things we wanted to say, and we have seen the academic women listening to us. We do not need a few women to speak for us, we can talk for ourselves and prefer to be able to directly participate and raise issues that concern us as women. It has been a great experience and a unique opportunity for me to participate in this forum. We have to continue in this direction. It is important for all the women, and I want to take the opportunity now to ask women like you three, with such recognition, to continue in this way, working with us and promoting this kind of forum.

※※※

I would like to ask you, Judith, about your intervention this morning concerning the "other women." You took a critical stance about the need to include the voices of other "other women," or women who are on the margins. I am particularly thinking here about the case of prostitutes. To what extent can nomenclature like that be accepted in the feminist movement? Or, in other words, is this debate accepted or acceptable somehow in the feminist movement?

BUTLER: I do think that there are now many organizations of prostitutes who have become part of the feminist movement and who have insisted on rights of unionization. In the U.S. there are unionization efforts everywhere. Also in Germany, I understand they had a march recently because there was a negative comment about prostitutes in a recent political debate and there were a thousand prostitutes in the street saying, "Don't use our name." So there is certainly a feminist movement of prostitutes, defending labor rights. Some women who are prostitutes will tell you that they make better money on the street than they ever could in the office. In fact, some choose to be there because it allows them to take care of their families or to realize their other goals. So, they shouldn't be simply victimized. There is one wing of the feminist movement that insists on understanding prostitution as a situation of pure victimization. They say, "Nobody would choose this, this is a terrible situation for women," but many prostitutes have said, "This is not true, this is my work and what I need is protection on the job. I need better wages, I need insurance, I need protection from physical violence." They have gone to collectives, which I believe are feminist, in order to achieve those goals. This is an extremely important political movement. However, at the same time, feminism opposes sexual violence, and I think there are forced slave trades or forced situations of prostitution that must be opposed, precisely because they are coerced.

⁂

And the case of transsexuals?

BUTLER: Well, you know, I think it is important for the feminist movement to organize in the name of women. But it is also important for the feminist movement to ask itself what it is to be a woman, who is a woman, what does it mean to become a woman. If you accept the notion that "woman" is a social category, that it has social meanings, then it is not always tied to a biological situation of being female. I think that transsexuality helps to understand the sex/gender distinction. I think you have this distinction in the Spanish language. This is an important topic, not only because transsexuals tend to suffer because of their gender and women have always suffered because of their gender, but because it helps us to understand the whole range of human, gendered experience. We must not be afraid of knowing what gender is, or how it is lived.

⧓

I would like to know exactly where, when, and how the concept of "dialogic feminism" was generated?

PUIGVERT: Actually, we generated this concept beginning with the work carried out with these women, the nonacademic women. Furthermore, the term "dialogic feminism" is due to the importance of establishing feminism for the twenty-first century in accordance with the society in which we live, and in accordance with the calls of all women who live in this society. That is to say, dialogic feminism comes from the very demand of those in the women's movement, when they claim that feminism should open up to the voices of all women, by means of egalitarian dialogue. This is really a new concept that reflects the dialogic turn that is currently spreading to most social spheres. It is starting to be a key concept on an international level, although we have already been using it for a while.

⧓

You have talked about a process that goes from victimization to transformation, and I would like to know whether you see any point of inflection on passing from one concept to the other.

BECK-GERNSHEIM: When we talk about transformation, there is a concept needed: agency. I think that the point of inflection is located at the moment women become agents. Women are agents, they are not just victims. They have knowledge, they know about options, and they try to make the best out of the very bad conditions they must sometimes face. They have to live with these conditions, they try to transform these conditions and this is how they become agents.

BUTLER: That's right, and I think we saw that, for instance, when Emilia talked about the Gypsies, and about her struggle for Gypsy girls, she said that Gypsy girls should have an education and that she must find a way to help them get in school, but to make sure that they also keep their culture. Within her struggle, Emilia is wondering how schools should change so that her culture is included and represented. On the one hand, the Gypsies are obviously disenfranchised, but Emilia is constantly fighting against this situation. I believe this is a remarkable experience of empowerment. She cannot read but she has a lot to say and to do. Then we saw the case of literacy. It is clear to me that this is a major problem, but what we saw there in the conference, I think quite beautifully, was how a social organization which helps especially women to learn how to read can produce women who have a certain pride. When Estrella [one of the women attending lieracy] read, it seemed to me that this was a beautiful moment, because we saw the transformation of the situation of disenfranchisement. Estrella's disenfranchisement was transformed into an experience of capacity. Throughout this conference we have been witnessing moments of transformation, which is not to deny serious disenfranchisement, nor to simply stay fixated on all the ways in which we are oppressed. It is instead to do something, to do something about it.

LEBRÓN: I would like to highlight the importance of dialogue and the way we have been learning literacy through dialogue, like Estrella demonstrated there. In these two days of conference we have seen how we are bringing our apprenticeships into practice. To speak up in public is not an easy thing to do. In fact, it is a really difficult situation. However, those of us who have experienced the practice of dialogue within our experience of literacy have been able to speak up here. Dialogic learning makes possible women's transformations and this is what Estrella read and this is the experience for many of us who found a space, a school, where we count. In this conference we could speak because here we count.

❈❈❈

PUIGVERT: Just to insist on one issue Judith mentioned in relation to the point of inflection: We, the women who have shared
the forum during these two days, have shown that we not only
speak about inequality and oppression, but we also announce
how to overcome them both. I think in the conference we have
significantly demonstrated that we can transform this situation
of inequality and oppression.

❈❈❈

*I would like to ask you, how is globalization affecting the femi-
nist movement? Is it strengthening the movement or not?*

BECK-GERNSHEIM: Well, the answer, in my eyes, is that there is
not one feminist movement—there are, rather, different voices
within the feminist movement. It is a democracy, not an autoc-
racy. So, as Judith said before, there are different voices within
the feminist movement, and they take different stances with regard to globalization. I mean, of course, that there are many
women within the feminist movement who think that globalization is very bad. I am different on that point. I think it is danger-
ous, but it does not have to be bad. We can do something with
it—we must do a globalization of social transformation. We are
also not just victims of globalization. That is important to me. I
do not know whether that is the answer you would give, so
maybe the other voices come in here. That was my voice, and
there are different voices.

❈❈❈

BUTLER: I would just add two things. Globalization has produced
a new challenge for transnational feminism, and we can see this
in struggles over corporate wages, as the corporations in question
are global, not simply local. There is one account of globalization
which says that "all the world is becoming the same," that it is
simply one large homogenizing effect, you know, McDonaldiz-
ing. But there is another account of globalization which says that

globalization is experienced differently in different parts of the world and that we must always ask what the local experience is. I would say that feminism has to ask what effect globalization has, especially on women's wages, which I think is a very, very important question, and on Third World countries, where there are not the same labor laws protecting women against excessive hours of work. However, I would also say that globalization makes it extremely important that we, feminists, find out more about the concrete lives of other women who are being affected by global processes, and that we must move between the global and the local, again and again, in order to not impose a single notion of feminism across.

❈

LEBRÓN: I agree with what Judith was saying about globalization, as it represents an opportunity for different women to know each other and to share things with each other. It does not have to consist of transforming other people's culture, our culture, my culture. Instead, globalization is an opportunity for getting to know and helping each other, and therefore it allows us to get to know that our culture is not *the* unique culture. There are others. For example, new technologies help social movements and associations to connect to each other and to be able to know what other movements or other groups are doing. In this way, they contribute to the different existing approaches and are open to learn from what other social movements are doing.

❈

In the present multicultural societies, do you think the Western feminist movement sees the arrival of other traditions, beliefs, and ways of living as a threat? I mean, do you think it can be a threat to the achievements feminism has reached?

BECK-GERNSHEIM: Rather than a threat, I would say it is a challenge. It is a challenge to see the world not just from our Western eyes. And I can give you a very concrete example: There is an image in Germany of "the real oppressed" woman: a Turkish woman wearing a *hijab*. The idea is that they are pushed by their parents into forced marriages, that their life is hard, and they have no options. And this is simply not the truth. This is just a very simplistic picture! It is true that some of them are forced by their parents to wear the *hijab,* but others want to do it, they give good reasons, and they can articulate these reasons. But to feminists in Germany, the *hijab* is still the symbol of oppression and they simply will not listen to the different voices from these women. They are now slowly, but very slowly, starting to realize this, but still too often they think, "oh, poor Turkish girl!" and do not listen to the Turkish girls saying, "no, look! It is not like this." If they do not listen, there is no dialogue.

❦

BUTLER: I would just say that the challenge for a transnational feminism is that we must not take Western feminism as a norm, as a truth. Our challenge is a question of cultural translation and a question of dialogue. We must see in what ways women express their desires, their aims, their hopes for themselves, what their concerns are, and we must learn that there isn't a single model which can govern freedom, or a single model of equality which can govern all women everywhere.

❦

PUIGVERT: Just to add that in this conference, we have seen that there is one step that needs to be taken by feminism: to look for the possibilities of an international dialogue, so that we can reformulate what some of us have thought about feminism. But this time we must do it differently. We need to reformulate feminist theory with the "other women," who did not take part in this dialogue before, who had been silenced and made invisible to feminism.

Note

1. Ana Lebrón is the president of the Federation of Cultural and Adult Education Associations (FACEPA). She is one of the Other Women who participated in the Conference.

Index

Studies in the Postmodern Theory of Education

General Editors
Joe L. Kincheloe & Shirley R. Steinberg

Counterpoints publishes the most compelling and imaginative books being written in education today. Grounded on the theoretical advances in criticalism, feminism, and postmodernism in the last two decades of the twentieth century, Counterpoints engages the meaning of these innovations in various forms of educational expression. Committed to the proposition that theoretical literature should be accessible to a variety of audiences, the series insists that its authors avoid esoteric and jargonistic languages that transform educational scholarship into an elite discourse for the initiated. Scholarly work matters only to the degree it affects consciousness and practice at multiple sites. Counterpoints' editorial policy is based on these principles and the ability of scholars to break new ground, to open new conversations, to go where educators have never gone before.

For additional information about this series or for the submission of manuscripts, please contact:

> Joe L. Kincheloe & Shirley R. Steinberg
> c/o Peter Lang Publishing, Inc.
> 275 Seventh Avenue, 28th floor
> New York, New York 10001

To order other books in this series, please contact our Customer Service Department:

> (800) 770-LANG (within the U.S.)
> (212) 647-7706 (outside the U.S.)
> (212) 647-7707 FAX

Or browse online by series:

> www.peterlangusa.com